Richard Wiggan has long been interes[illegible] the sea and ships. He was in the Sea Cadets during the Second World War and had ambitions to enter the Royal Navy as a signaller. Instead he found himself conscripted into Ernest Bevin's 'army' as a Bevin Boy, destined for almost four years in the mines. When working in the pits he felt the urge to write and formed an ambition to be a journalist. For many years a reporter and editor of various weekly newspapers, he has also written extensively for numerous magazines and is the author of several books. He has three sons and lives in the picturesque Ribble Valley of his native Lancashire.

May you have calm seas and a safe haven on lifes voyage.

Richard

March 1993

HUNT the *ALTMARK*

by

Richard Wiggan

ROBERT HALE · LONDON

First published in Great Britain 1982
Paperback edition 1990

Robert Hale Limited
Clerkenwell House
Clerkenwell Green
London EC1R 0HT

ISBN 0 7090 4254 X

Set by Rowland Phototypesetting Limited
Printed in Great Britain by St Edmundsbury Press Limited,
Bury St Edmunds, Suffolk and bound by Hunter & Foulis

Contents

List of Illustrations

Acknowledgments

One of the pleasures of writing this book has been that of finding so many people willing to give of their time and patience in helping to get at the truth of the *Altmark* affair. I am especially indebted to William Melville-Evans, former third officer of the *Doric Star*, sunk by the *Admiral Graf Spee*, and to Captain Walter Schmidt, former third officer of the *Altmark*. Without the assistance they so willingly gave in answering my seemingly endless questions, both in person and by post, this book would never have been written. It was also a privilege for me to be instrumental in bringing them together so long after that night in Jossingfjord. I am greatly indebted also to Mr Stanley Wells, of Hobart, Tasmania, for allowing me to draw on material left by his late brother, Mr W. F. Wells, seventh engineer of the *Tairoa*, which was another of the ships sunk by the *Admiral Graf Spee*. I am grateful also to Commander Bradwell Talbot Turner, R.N. (retd), who was second in command of H.M.S. *Cossack*, for putting me right over the famous cry "The Navy's here!"

Many Norwegians have helped by providing information, both from a personal point of view and otherwise. Of these, I am pleased to acknowledge help so unstintingly given by Major H. Vassbo (retd), of Sandnes, and by the Norwegian writer Gerd Schanche, also of Sandnes. My thanks are due also to Inge S. Arstad, of Stavanger, for allowing me use of a translation of a letter written by his brother, the late Sigurd S. Arstad, to their father concerning the *Altmark* affair. Sigurd Arstad was then a captain in the Norwegian Navy at Bergen.

In this connection, too, I must thank Commodore Harald B. M. Ronneberg, editor of *Norsk Militaert Tidsskrift*, and also for his comments arising from personal experience of events while the *Altmark* was in Norwegian waters. For a sea pilot's view of events aboard the *Altmark* after she left Jossingfjord, I am in the debt of Lars Rimereid, of Stavanger, who related the experiences of his father-in-law, Oscar Olsen. Lt-Col. Knut M. Haugland, Director, Norges Hjemmefrontmuseum, Akershus, Oslo, also assisted, and the editor of the *Stavanger Aftenblad* helped by publishing my request for information.

I must stress my debt to the staff of the Public Record Office at Kew for help in researching the British Admiralty account of the *Altmark* affair, covered in file ADM 199/281, and also make acknowledgment for drawing on the papers for background purposes and for permission to list in Appendix 1 the names of the released prisoners.

Finally, I would like to thank World Ship Society colleague Hans Graf, of Hamburg, who did so much to lay the foundations for my research in West Germany. The society's Central Record was a mine of information on individual ships.

Author's note

Readers may perhaps wonder how it is that so long after the events described I am able, in some instances, to quote conversations as they took place at the time. To avoid any misunderstanding, I would point out that they are based on actual accounts given to me by survivors and participants, either in person, in writing, or from records they kept. Other reported conversations arise from accounts in official records.

For my mother and my sons
Also Margaret, who believed

Prologue

In a bleak Norwegian fjord on a mid-February night in 1940, there was enacted what came to be regarded as one of the most stirring episodes of the opening months of the Second World War. It had everything to stir the imagination of the British nation at a time when the people were in need of something to boost their morale. It was the phoney war period, and what was happening seemed to be going the Germans' way. Gunther Prien, commander of the *U-47*, had cocked a snook at the Royal Navy a little over a month after the outbreak of war by sneaking into Scapa Flow, where he torpedoed the battleship *Royal Oak* as she rode at anchor. He then conned the *U-47* out of the Navy's own backyard and returned to Germany to be acclaimed a hero.

In the South Atlantic, the German pocket battleship the *Admiral Graf Spee* had roamed in search of merchant ships sailing alone. She kept popping up here and there like a Scarlet Pimpernel of the ocean before finally being run to ground and scuttled at Montevideo after the Battle of the River Plate in December 1939. The event made world headlines, but she had left behind "mother"—her supply ship, the tanker *Altmark*. What was more important was the fact that held in the tanker's holds were the crews of merchant ships sunk by the *Graf Spee*.

The scuttling of the *Graf Spee*, the cause of rejoicing in Britain, had greatly relieved the pressure on the British Navy, whose hunting groups had been tied up seeking the raider, at first thought to be the *Admiral Scheer*. The Naval forces were now free to "scrub and search" the South Atlantic for the *Altmark*.

The tanker, alone and with every ship a potential foe, lurked in the wastes of the South Atlantic until making a dash for Germany with the odds against her. She reached Norway and, with a little more luck, might well have got back to Germany. She had on board 299 British merchant seamen, some of whom had been captives since October 1939. The prisoners were a source of great concern to Captain Heinrich Dau, master of the *Altmark*. He did not want them in the first place, but obviously a fighting ship such as the *Admiral Graf Spee* could not accommodate them. The *Graf Spee* had, in fact, been so short of space herself that her crew was reduced prior to her sailing from Germany before the outbreak of war.

Dau had no option but to take them, and they were imprisoned in "flats" in the *Altmark*. Conditions were not good. It was those conditions that gave rise to stories of a "hell-ship" and monster of a captain after the destroyer H.M.S. *Cossack* intercepted the *Altmark* in Jossingfjord and dashed back to Leith with the rescued men. Those in the dockside waiting to provide aid were surprised to see that the men could walk unaided and were not suffering from starvation and ill-treatment as had been expected. They were, however, not exactly a picture of health after months of confinement. Their faces were pale due to spending long hours below decks and they had lost weight, but, everything considered, they had stood up to their experiences well. Food was of the plainest, but, according to one survivor, no worse than he had known as an apprentice at sea.

But throughout the voyage there was a duel of wits between captives and captors. Dau had the aid of guards provided by the *Graf Spee* to keep watch over the prisoners. Many of the officers from the captured ships had been kept on board the pocket battleship before being released at Montevideo. Still, more than fifty ships' officers remained in the *Altmark*, and several of the navigating officers were able to plot the *Altmark*'s voyage from the South Atlantic on a chart they kept in secret.

The crew of the *Altmark* were mostly from Hamburg and not Nazis. They had sailed the oceans of the world between them and were less likely to be influenced by Nazism. The guards from the *Graf Spee* were young and of a different generation, brought up under Nazism and followers of Hitler.

The commander of the pocket battleship, Captain Hans Langsdorff, was of another school. He observed standards of conduct that were to have no part in the grim warfare that was to be waged in the North Atlantic and on the convoy run to Russia. He maintained a strict and correct attitude in his dealings with his prisoners. On one occasion he apologized to his captives and had them entertained to a Sunday afternoon concert on board the pocket battleship.

He died by his own hand after scuttling his ship rather than risk further loss of life. There are some, however, who argue that he should have fought it out, maintaining that the ship was not too badly damaged. None can doubt his bravery. It takes a man of courage to die in the manner Langsdorff did after writing letters and wrapping himself in an ensign of the old Imperial German Navy before committing the final act.

Controversy also surrounded the boarding of the *Altmark* in Norwegian waters. The Norwegians did not forgive the captain of the *Cossack*, Captain Philip Vian (later to be Admiral of the Fleet Sir Philip Vian), as he was to learn some years after the end of the war. The prisoners were, in fact, entitled to release once the *Altmark* entered Norwegian territorial waters, these being neutral waters.

The Norwegians later claimed the *Altmark* had been "inspected". This, of course, is different from "searched", which may have given rise to misunderstanding at the time. The British were under the impression that the *Altmark* had been searched. As this had not revealed the prisoners reported to be on board, they determined to find out for themselves. It was Winston Churchill who, as First Lord of the Admiralty, settled the matter by giving instructions that led to the boarding of the *Altmark* after Norwegian protests had been ignored. Norway did not like it, but soon there were more important things to concern the Norwegians, for in April of 1940 the Germans invaded their country.

Men who had been prisoners in the *Altmark* went to other ships. Some were to lose their lives in those ships, while the *Altmark* was herself to meet an untimely end. But the legend remains. . . .

1

The Lamp Does Not Burn

Bank Holiday, August 1939—the last peacetime Bank Holiday the British were to enjoy for six years, although they did not know that as they relaxed in deckchairs or strolled the promenades. The holiday got off to a dull start at Blackpool, but the sun broke through and the thousands of visitors in the northern resort relaxed happily on the sands or trod the famous Golden Mile. The story was the same at other resorts around the British coast. The people were happy if a little uncertain about the future, but had not Prime Minister Neville Chamberlain returned from Munich eleven months earlier waving a piece of paper and exclaiming, "Peace for our time"?

The Munich Agreement had been signed on 30th September 1938 between Great Britain, France, Germany and Italy, under which Czechoslovakia had to cede to Germany the Sudetenland, mainly inhabited by Germans. Some considered the agreement a sell-out, but whatever the rights and wrongs of the issue it bought Britain time. The fact that that time was running out was, however, forgotten for the moment as the British relaxed on what, for many of them, was to be the last peacetime Bank Holiday they were to see.

While the holidaymakers enjoyed themselves, a black and grey-hulled tanker lay berthed at Kiel, Germany, sailing time only hours away. Big quantities of food, most of it canned, had been taken on board. Stores, welding and diving equipment, drum upon drum of lubrication oil and other materials vanished into her holds. There was no thought of holiday among her crew as more and more stores were hoisted aboard. Apart from the vast amount of supplies, another factor marked her out as a vessel of more than ordinary significance—secreted away, and hidden by stores, was a 15-centimetre gun, with ammunition.

The tanker was the *Altmark*, built by Howaldts-Werke, A. G. Kiel, launched on 13th November 1937, and commissioned on 14th November 1938. She had a gross tonnage of 10,847 and a deadweight capacity of 14,137 tons. Her displacement fully laden was 22,350 tons.

Her four double-acting two-stroke nine-cylinder M.A.N. engines gave a total of 21,400 h.p. and a speed of 21 knots. Her length overall was 178 metres with a beam of 22 metres. She had been well tested on exercises in the North Atlantic and the Mediterranean when she carried two and sometimes three 15-centimetre guns.

The crew understood that the *Altmark* was to load a cargo of light diesel oil in America, and afterwards would supply a German Navy ship, perhaps a cruiser, during a world-wide voyage. It was true in part, but her full role remained a secret.

Captain Heinrich Dau, the *Altmark*'s master, was not a man to be popular with his crew. His manner was austere, but his career was one that merited respect. He had worked his way up to be a captain with the North German Lloyd, and later became captain of several big passenger liners of the Hamburg-Amerika Line until 1938. He had been a German Navy Officer in the First World War, and the discipline and manner of the old naval tradition remained with him. He was strict and inclined to be harsh, with a desire to dominate. Yet he had a high regard for experienced sailors whatever their nationality.

Walter Schmidt, the 26-year-old third officer of the *Altmark*, saw another side of his captain when, in the month before the *Altmark* was due to sail, he asked Dau to sign him off in order that he could study for his master's certificate. Dau told him: "Sorry, Mr Schmidt, I need you for the next few months, but when you can change the policies of Mr Hitler, you can leave and take your master's licence."

Schmidt kept the remarks to himself, for he knew that should he report them, then Dau would probably be sent to a concentration camp. Nobody who valued his life uttered what in the Germany of the time could be regarded as treason against the state.

Dau had as his chief officer Friedrich Paulsen, a submariner in the First World War, while the chief engineer was Schleusner, with Ott second engineer. Second officers were de Harde, Schroder, Rummler and Garte. The posts of wireless operators were filled by Thurz, Wendt and Luka.

Perhaps the one man who stood out from the other officers was the ship's doctor, Rudolf Tyrolt, who was to play an important part in the months ahead. His was an outgoing personality and his position as ship's doctor was yet another in the varied jobs he had held after studying at university. He had spent most of his life in America and the Argentine, turning his hand to various occupations, including fishing and journalism. Once he had done a voyage as a fireman on a coal-burning ship. He was not a man to let things get him down.

So it was that on Sunday, 6th August 1939, with the Bank Holiday in Britain at its height, the *Altmark* left her berth at Kiel. Each member of the crew, alone with his thoughts, wondered when he would see Germany again. Walter Schmidt, married only in May of that year, was thinking of the young bride he had left behind. Tyrolt was as usual looking ahead to new adventures, but others were thinking of their families and friends. Captain Dau, on the bridge, though married with a family, had no time for sentiment as the *Altmark* headed for the open sea. His face, sporting a grey goatee beard that was later to earn him the name of "Knitty Whiskers", showed no emotion as he rapped out orders. Their destination was Port Arthur, Texas, where they were to load 15,000 tons of light diesel oil. The *Altmark* passed through the English Channel and attracted but little interest. The English were enjoying their Bank Holiday Sunday.

The voyage to America was uneventful, the *Altmark* arriving at Port Arthur on 17th August. The diesel fuel was loaded, but just as Dau was hoping to be able to leave without delay he ran into difficulties. "The Americans are suspicious," he told his officers. The Customs and Coast Guard wanted to search the ship, but Dau knew that if they did this thoroughly, then *Altmark*'s true role would be revealed. He allowed them only to inspect the accommodation and to see the loaded cargo tanks. He also contacted the German Consul, and after further wrangling the *Altmark* was allowed to leave on 19th August, ostensibly bound for Europe.

The *Altmark* sailed on, her crew, all civilians, now settled into a routine, chatting about what was to be their last trip on shore for a long time. Two days out from Port Arthur, Dau received a wireless message from Berlin that sent a ripple of rumour throughout the ship. The message read: "Danger for war." Dau immediately ordered a change of course.

Tension was mounting, and then four days later Dau received another message: "*Steuerbordlampe brennt nicht mehr*". This, translated, read "Starboard lamp does not burn" and meant, out of code, "Very great danger for war. Keep out of all traffic."

As the *Altmark* kept out of the traffic lanes, awaiting new instructions by the hour, another ship had slipped out of Germany. She was the pocket battleship the *Admiral Graf Spee*, bound for the Atlantic.

The *Graf Spee* was one of three pocket battleships built by the

Germans that very cleverly got round the limitations imposed by the Versailles Treaty. They exceeded the treaty limit of 10,000 tons by about 2,000 tons. Their armament included 11-inch guns and they had a top speed of 28 knots. They also had a long range.

The other pocket battleships were the *Deutschland* and the *Admiral Scheer*. Their role was that of raiders on the high seas, dodging about the oceans like grey ghosts, striking a sudden blow then vanishing again.

The value of a raider lies not so much in the number of ships she sinks, but in the uncertainty she causes. The enemy is never sure where or when she will strike and so naval forces that would normally be engaged on other duties are tied down hunting the raider.

The advantage is with the raider. She can disappear at will immediately after a sinking. Merchantmen sailing independently are at her mercy, for whatever armament they carry—if any—is useless once a raider sights her prey. Her spotter aircraft will have reported the victim before she is even aware of it. The victim may get off a raider report but if she does that then she runs the risk of being shot out of the water with consequent loss of life. At the best, her radio cabin can be destroyed, also with possible loss of life, and before a message can be sent. In any event, getting off a message will not help the victim, though it may alert hunting groups.

The raider must avoid engagement with enemy units unless it is unavoidable. For there is no value in sinking an enemy warship if she herself is crippled in the process. The raider must at all costs remain intact, and one thing she must be sure of is supplies. For this it is essential to have a ship which, loaded with supplies, will meet the raider at secretly arranged spots and supply her with stores and fuel and perhaps also take on board prisoners from ships sunk by the raider.

It was for such a role that the *Altmark* was cast. She was to play "mother" to the *Graf Spee*, which, the last of the three pocket battleships to be completed, sailed from Wilhelmshaven on the evening of 21st August 1939. She took evasive action when any other ships were sighted, and on 28th August received a message from Berlin, giving instructions for a meeting with the *Altmark*. The *Graf Spee*, again avoiding all shipping, set course for the waiting area near the Cape Verde Islands, off the coast of West Africa. The meeting was fixed for 1st September.

On board the *Altmark*, there was no longer any doubt about the tanker's role. Some of the vast quantity of paint she had taken aboard was put to use to change the appearance of the *Altmark*. The crew began painting the ship yellow. Hull, masts, funnel, deck and hatches were all painted to disguise the tanker. She then became the *Sogne*, with Oslo as her home port. The Norwegian flag was also flown so that the suspicions of any British warship that came upon them would be allayed. At the same time, Dau had preparations made for burning and sinking the ship in case the ruse did not succeed.

It was a trying time for the third officer, Schmidt. He had been a radio operator in several cargo ships from 1936 to 1937, and had an operator's licence. Dau, anxious for all the latest news and to have at hand at once any messages that came from S.K.L.—Seekriegsleitung—in Berlin, drove Schmidt hard. The third officer was on duty in the wireless cabin from midnight until six in the morning and from noon for another six hours. Dau also wanted every scrap of news that could be gleaned from foreign radio stations.

Dau knew, despite what he might say to his officers and crew, that from the naval point of view war was coming earlier than had been anticipated. Grand Admiral Erich Raeder, who was appointed commander-in-chief of the German Navy in 1928, had originally thought that war with Britain would start in the mid-1940s, but by 1938 was having second thoughts, and what was known as the Z Plan was drawn up, which included in the programme the delivery of large battleships within six years, two to four years earlier than originally estimated. The idea had been at first to go for a balanced fleet, but the Z Plan aimed at an offensive and powerful force as soon as possible. Even so, there was still a narrow margin of time, and, as it turned out, it was not enough.

Sailing under the Norwegian flag, the *Altmark* forged ahead, the gap between herself and the *Graf Spee* narrowing by the hour. Dau studied his orders, and discussed with Paulsen the arrangements for meeting the pocket battleship. There would be plenty to do in the transfer of stores and fuel. All the time a keen watch must be kept for other ships. They did not want the operation to be doomed before it had even had a chance to begin.

Third Officer Schmidt was snatching what rest he could between being on watch in the radio room and answering Dau's constant demands to know what was happening. The engineers were nursing the engines and seeing that they kept running sweetly. It was vital that they did for the *Altmark* would have to depend largely on her speed and disguise to avoid detection. Dr Tyrolt was checking his small stock of medical supplies, and hoping that he would not be called upon to meet any real emergency or serious outbreak of illness.

In the crew's quarters, the men discussed the war they now realized was inevitable. The other men had left behind wives and grown-up families, while some of the younger men had just started married life. They had left wives and young children, and wondered when they would see them again. The men with sons old enough for military service hoped that they would survive whatever lay ahead.

Would Britain and France declare war on Germany if she marched into Poland? The crew debated the question as they ate or relaxed between watches. There were mixed feelings. Many of the crew had friends in England and America. They chanced upon each other at their various ports of call. Now all that was over. They would be enemies if they met again, and many would perish once the war began in earnest. None of the older men at least looked forward to the coming war.

"This is it." Dau stabbed a point on the chart. "This is where we will meet the *Graf Spee*." He indicated an area near the Cape Verde Islands. He had received a message stating where the *Altmark* was to meet up with the pocket battleship on 1st September.

Paulsen nodded in agreement as Dau strutted about enlarging on the arrangements. They had, he said, an important duty. They must keep the *Graf Spee* well provisioned and supplied with fuel. The *Altmark* must be content to serve in a passive role.

"But," Dau went on, "we must be ever vigilant. The task with which we have been entrusted is a vital one. Remember this. If for any reason we fail, then the *Graf Spee*, without supplies and fuel, will be at the mercy of our enemies. Well supplied, she can roam the ocean and inflict losses without fear of too much harm to herself.

"The *Graf Spee* will have surprise on her side. She will be able to strike and then disappear before any harm can come to her."

"Herr Kapitaen, but what if she is intercepted by a British cruiser, or if we are caught?"

Dau swung round on the young officer who had had the temerity to interrupt him and, holding his temper with difficulty, said: "The *Graf Spee* is a match for the British. But her task is not to fight, but to serve as a raider. Yet if she is trapped, then she will fight, and fight well. We ourselves must rely on speed and on our disguises, and we shall not be short of these during the voyage that lies ahead of us."

He smiled indulgently, and then his mood became brisk. "It will not be long now before we meet the *Graf Spee*. We must keep extra alert as we near the meeting area. See that the crew do not relax their vigilance. To your duties, gentlemen."

The officers filed out. The *Altmark* pushed through the ocean, the last hours of peace slipping away.

2

Ocean Rendezvous

A high swell was running as the morning of 1st September dawned. All was excitement on board the *Altmark*. "Not long now," Paulsen commented as the eager lookouts scanned the horizon. It was a peaceful scene out there in the Atlantic, but at 5.30, European time, that morning the German Army had marched on Poland while German bombers rained death and destruction on her cities and towns. The *Altmark* seemed to have no connection with the scenes of horror that were being enacted at that moment in Poland.

Suddenly there was a shout from the lookout. "Mast in sight!" Dau wondered for a moment if they had been spotted by an enemy ship. He trained his binoculars on the distant mast. A signal stabbed out from the ship that was now approaching rapidly. Dau relaxed slightly. It was the recognition signal from the *Graf Spee*. On a pinpoint of ocean, "mother" and the warship that she was to succour had met at last.

If Dau had been anxious, then so too was Captain Langsdorff in the *Graf Spee*. A few minutes after 8 a.m., a lookout had reported two masts in sight. Langsdorff had a moment of anxiety that the vessel might be a British warship. He was reassured when the report came that it was a tanker. Recognition was established, and the first hurdle was now over. The *Altmark* had been sighted in 24° 25′ north, 36° 15′ west, and now the two ships were riding close by each other, with preparations being made for the transfer of fuel and stores.

The crew of the *Altmark* admired the majestic picture the *Graf Spee* made as she rode in the swell. For their part, the *Graf Spee* sailors were looking with curiosity at the *Altmark*, flying the Norwegian flag in her guise as the *Sogne*.

The high swell made it difficult to ferry across the anti-aircraft guns and ammunition, foodstuffs and general supplies. A pipe-line was also connected up, and fuel began to flow from the *Altmark* to the *Graf Spee*.

There was also the transfer to the *Altmark* of about twenty men to handle the anti-aircraft guns, and two wireless operators. The officer in charge, also transferred from the *Graf Spee*, was Lieutenant Otto Schmidt, whose youthful appearance was later to earn him the nickname of "Babyface" from prisoners in the *Altmark*. There was no thought then of accommodating prisoners, and the naval personnel were there merely to handle the armament and to help with wireless traffic. There were two other officers from the *Graf Spee* in addition to Otto Schmidt. They were Wegener, who as purser officer was to be responsible for the stores carried in the *Altmark* for the *Graf Spee*, and Weichert, prize officer. Both had been reserve officers before the war. The *Altmark* was now carrying more than one hundred men.

While all this was going on, Dau had been taken across to the battleship to meet Langsdorff and discuss future operations. Langsdorff greeted him correctly, but coolly. Dau met the senior officers, including Kay, the second in command. Dau was accustomed to remaining aloof, but now it was his turn to be overawed as Langsdorff politely but firmly outlined his plans. War had still not been declared, and it was agreed that *Altmark* should keep company with the *Graf Spee*.

As Dau returned to the tanker, his boat passed through a busy scene. The sun shone down warmly as the fuel was pumped across to the *Graf Spee* and stores ferried across. There was, however, something almost sinister about the clandestine operation. The scene looked peaceful enough, but had another ship chanced upon the lonely meeting place, news of the *Graf Spee* would not have been long reaching the British Admiralty in London.

Anxious eyes scanned the sky and the horizon as the work went ahead. It was also essential that no rubbish remain on the surface. A wooden case or general flotsam would alert other vessels to the presence of the pocket battleship. This fear was one that was to be a constant source of anxiety to Dau and his officers later. Now orders were rapped out to the seamen manning the boats to make certain that nothing was left bobbing about in the swell. The men sweated and cursed in the warm sunshine.

That night, as the two ships kept company, the opportunity was taken to test the blackout arrangements of the *Graf Spee* and *Altmark*. Only a chink of light was necessary to disclose their presence to a passing ship. The *Altmark*'s wireless operators had been reinforced from the *Graf Spee*, and a constant vigil was kept on broadcasts from Europe, which seemed remote as the two ships sailed southward. The weather was daily becoming warmer. Both Langsdorff and Dau made full use of the chance afforded to exercise the crews in their various duties. Dau ordered exercises with the lifeboat and to go over yet again the preparations for burning or sinking the ship should they meet with a British or French warship.

Yet the question remained—when would war come? Would the British and French keep their promise to Poland now that Germany had marched into that country? This was a question pondered on both ships. Third Officer Schmidt thought frequently of his young wife and of how she was faring. Dau continued to play the role of martinet. He lacked the quiet authority of Langsdorff and was inclined to hector. He, too, pondered on whether Britain would again declare war on Germany. He looked at the calendar—the date said 2nd September.

When 3rd September dawned, it promised another warm day as the *Graf Spee* and *Altmark* continued to sail southward and into still warmer weather. The crews went about their duties, and then came the news in a radiogram from Berlin, but the British Admiralty had already broadcast in plain language: "11 a.m. Commence hostilities at once against Germany." This message was picked up by the *Graf Spee* before the Berlin message was received. The pre-arranged message "Total Germany" was sent by the Admiralty to British naval craft.

In Britain, Sunday morning worshippers were listening on radios taken into church to Prime Minister Neville Chamberlain spelling out in grave tones the announcement that Great Britain was again at war with Germany, for the second time in a little over twenty years. He said, as men left their gardens or abandoned their Sunday morning walk to listen:

> I am speaking to you from the Cabinet Room at 10 Downing Street. This morning the British Ambassador in Berlin handed the German Government a final Note, stating that unless we heard from them by eleven o'clock that they were prepared at once to withdraw their troops from Poland a state of war would exist between us. I have to tell you now that no such undertaking has been received and that consequently this country is at war with Germany.

A man who was to play an important role in the subsequent affair of the *Altmark* was appointed First Lord of the Admiralty. He was Mr Winston Churchill, who had occupied that post in the First World War. The war was not many hours old when he received news of the sinking of the Donaldson Line passenger liner *Athenia*, just out from Britain on her way to Canada, by the *U-30*, commanded by Fritz-

Ludwig Lemp, who was apparently under the impression that the ship was an auxiliary cruiser.

The 1936 Submarine Agreement made it illegal for a submarine to sink a merchantman on sight. The prize laws must be observed. Passengers and crews must be put in a place of safety. A ship's boats were not considered a place of safety unless land or another vessel that could take them on board were nearby. They were laws that Langsdorff was to observe as the *Graf Spee* foraged in the South Atlantic. The *Altmark* was an enemy ship, of course, but it did offer some sort of safety for the crews of those ships sunk by the *Graf Spee*.

The prize laws meant that the U-boat commanders were literally fighting with one hand tied behind their backs if the submarines were to achieve their highest potential; and it was inevitable that as the sea war hotted up the restrictions would be ignored, as they were.

German ships at sea on the outbreak of war were taking no chances. Five German liners took refuge in Lobito Bay, Angola, then Portuguese West Africa. Merchant ships sought refuge in Latvian ports.

So as Europe made its uncertain way into another world war, the *Altmark* and *Graf Spee* seemed cut off from it all. Dau went busily about his plans for seeing that the *Altmark* fulfilled the role chosen for her. The tanker was still sailing in company with the *Graf Spee*. The crews of both ships took the opportunity to do some sunbathing, and for a time were able to forget the war in Europe.

It had been agreed that the pocket battleship should operate several hundred miles west of Freetown, but four days after the declaration of war, the *Graf Spee* was ordered by Berlin to move away from the operational area. The *Graf Spee* and "mother" then moved into what was considered to be the comparative safety of the South Atlantic wastes. But there was to be little safety anywhere for the marauder, and the *Graf Spee* and *Altmark* had a lucky escape from being spotted by a British cruiser, the *Cumberland*, and an unknown ship.

So time passed until Langsdorff was ordered to take the *Graf Spee* on her first sortie against merchant shipping. The battleship and the tanker parted company on 27th September, after a rendezvous had been arranged for 14th October.

The battleship was bound for an area off Brazil. It was then that the *Graf Spee*, like the *Altmark*, changed her identity. The name *Graf Spee* was painted out, and she became the *Admiral Scheer*. It was this that was to hoodwink the crews of ships subsequently sunk by the *Graf Spee* and to lead the British Admiralty to believe that the raider at large in the South Atlantic was the *Admiral Scheer*. The *Graf Spee*, in her new guise, headed for the region of Pernambuco.

In the *Altmark* it was now a matter of waiting. There was time to carry out exercises and to ensure that everything was ready in case of emergency. Dau was testy and seemed inclined to pick on Third Officer Schmidt. "Mr Schmidt," he said, "you are one of the youngest officers, and I want you to give instruction on how to shoot. You will get out revolvers and train ten of the men how to handle them." A target was accordingly put up and the calm of the South Atlantic was disturbed by the crack of revolver shots. It made a diversion for the Equator had been crossed without the traditional "Crossing of the Line" ceremony.

The real reason for training the men to use revolvers was because of Dau's fear of being intercepted by a British or French submarine.

Dau strode in front of the third officer and outlined his plan. "We must be ready, Mr Schmidt," said Dau, stroking his goatee. "It will be your job if we are stopped to go with the ten men in a boat with a bag containing papers and a big bottle of ether."

Schmidt gaped as Dau warmed towards the plan he had thought up and began enthusiastically to outline it. His idea was that Schmidt should go alongside the submarine and then, as the boat bumped against the submarine's side, he should grab the long rope already hidden in the boat and snap this to the submarine's rail. The rope would be fitted with a snapper in readiness.

With this done, Schmidt, under the guise of boarding the submarine, was to fling the bottle of ether down the conning tower, the *Altmark*'s sharpshooters in the boat in the meantime taking care to those members of the submarine's crew on the casing. Then, according to Dau's theory, the submarine, manned by men almost overcome by the ether, would try to dive.

They would be too confused to react properly, and the *Altmark* would be able to secure the submarine, Schmidt having paved the way with the rope, before she could dive. Anchors would then be used to hold the enemy craft captive.

Schmidt reeled under the madness of the idea and could only see himself dead, badly wounded, or at best taken prisoner by the submarine, if the crew did not blaze away in brutal retaliation, killing all of them in the boat. He was willing to serve the Fatherland, but this, he felt, was going beyond the duty of the third officer in a supply ship.

Dau also insisted that Schmidt supervise exercises with a lifeboat. "We must be ready, Mr Schmidt," Dau would keep repeating. So the lifeboat was launched, and the luckless crew, with the sun blazing down, would toil at the oars.

The other officers watched from the bridge as the boat was lowered. Schmidt and his men rowed away, the boat's crew sweating in the burning heat. The boat rose and fell in the swell, and as the toiling men looked longingly at their ship they thought of the cooling breeze that their comrades would be enjoying as the *Altmark* moved through the sea. For moving she was.

"What is happening?" one of the crew asked. Heads turned as the *Altmark* began to draw away. It was then nine in the morning, and soon their ship disappeared from sight.

"It is mad, mad," Schmidt thought to himself. What were they going to do out in the middle of the South Atlantic, just rowing to nowhere? It seemed ridiculous to him as they rowed on. The day died gradually, the crew quenching their thirst with the water they had brought with them and eating what little food they had.

Slowly the hours dragged by, until a shout went up, "There she is!" With relief they saw the *Altmark* approaching. It was then eight o'clock in the evening and they had been in the boat for eleven hours. The men's hands were sore with rowing and some of them were suffering from sunburn. They were also smarting under what they considered to be a useless operation. It was the worst day they had experienced in the rowing exercises.

"Excellent, Mr Schmidt," said Dau as the third officer reported to the captain before seeking refuge and rest in his cabin. "No one will catch us napping. We must be ready for whatever may happen."

"See that the men keep alert," he admonished Schmidt as the officer turned to go. The crew were in fact fully alert. Their glasses swept the sky for aircraft and the sea for ships or submarines. Three lookouts were stationed on each wing of the bridge, six on the compass deck and one in the mast.

The preparations for burning or sinking the ship in case of detection by the British or French were also gone over again and again. Dau did not want the *Altmark* to fall into enemy hands, and feared what the consequences would be for the *Graf Spee*, should she be deprived of "mother". "We must survive for the sake of the *Graf Spee*," he told Paulsen in a moment of confidence to his first officer. "It is our duty." He did not stop to ponder what would happen to the *Altmark* if the

Graf Spee met with disaster. He could not conceive—or dare not think—of such a thing happening.

Dau, though he would not admit it, was also seeking a slice of glory for himself. The ordering of Schmidt to train the men to shoot and to see that they kept up to scratch with rowing was all a means of giving Dau a chance to become a hero.

While Dau dreamed his own dreams of glory, the *Graf Spee* was on the brink of making her first "kill". It was 30th September when suddenly over the airwaves went the distress message "R.R.R.—*Clement* gunned." This meant that she was being attacked by a surface raider. The *Clement*, 5,050-ton steamer, was on passage from New York to Bahia, Salvador, carrying cases of kerosene.

She was off Pernambuco when she was spotted by the *Graf Spee*'s Arado aircraft. The third officer, H. J. Gill, who was on watch, saw a ship on the port bow. He identified it as a battleship heading straight for the *Clement*. Almost at once an aircraft swooped down, signalling the ship to stop and not to transmit. To add weight to her order, she followed it up by opening fire. The *Clement* stopped as the bullets thudded into the upperworks.

The master, Captain F. C. P. Harris, ordered the boats to be lowered. The R.R.R. signal was sent off, and the confidential books thrown overboard in the already weighted bag.

As the crew pulled away from the *Clement* a boat approached from the battleship. The capbands of the sailors bore the words "Admiral Scheer". "It's the *Admiral Scheer*," exclaimed one of the *Clement*'s crew. Langsdorff's ruse was working. The Germans took Captain Harris and his chief engineer, Mr W. Bryant, back on board the *Clement*, which was now wallowing in the swell. The chief engineer was ordered to open the sea-valves in the engine room. Meanwhile, the Germans placed explosives around the ship.

The captain and chief engineer were then taken to the *Graf Spee*. There they had their first glimpse of Langsdorff, who told Captain Harris that the *Clement* would have to be sunk. It was some satisfaction to Captain Harris and Mr Bryant that two torpedoes fired at the *Clement* missed, and that gunfire had to be resorted to before the *Clement* took her final plunge. It was a sad moment for the Merchant Navy officers. Langsdorff had expressed regret to Captain Harris about sinking his ship, saying: "It is war."

The Merchant Navy officers saw themselves as future prisoners-of-war, but almost three hours later another ship was sighted. This proved to be the *Papalemos*, a Greek and neutral. The *Graf Spee* ordered her to stop, and, to their surprise, Captain Harris and the chief engineer were transferred to her. The Greek was then allowed to proceed.

Langsdorff was also concerned that the rest of the crew of the *Clement* should be in no danger. He had a signal sent off to Olinda, the transmitting station at Pernambuco, asking that aid be given to the merchant ship's lifeboats. In this he was carrying out the prize laws in assuring as far as he could the safety of the crew of the *Clement*. It was also typical of the man himself.

The captain of the *Graf Spee* knew that by setting free the crew of the *Clement* and sending a signal to the radio station he was also putting his own ship at risk by disclosing to the world that a German raider was marauding in the South Atlantic. Thanks to the efforts at disguise, however, it was thought that the raider was the *Admiral Scheer*.

The British Admiralty had been waiting for just such an event, and on receiving the news they at once sprang into action. Subsequently, a number of hunting groups were formed. They comprised battleships, battle-cruisers, cruisers and aircraft carriers. It was again an indication of what one raider can do in draining naval resources needed urgently elsewhere.

Covering the North America and West Indies area were the cruisers *Berwick* and *York*, while the *Cumberland*, *Exeter*, *Ajax* and *Achilles* patrolled off the east coast of South America. The *Sussex* and *Shropshire* were to cover the Cape of Good Hope area, with the cruisers *Cornwall* and *Dorsetshire*, along with the aircraft carrier *Eagle*, covering Ceylon. The *Renown* and *Ark Royal* were to operate between Pernambuco and Freetown. The remaining groups covered other areas. French ships were also involved in what in total amounted to nine groups and twenty-three ships. One group operated in the Indian Ocean. The snares were now out for the raider. Twist and turn as she might, it could not be long before, in one way or another, the trap was sprung. The battleships, cruisers and aircraft carriers cut through the water, endlessly searching for their elusive quarry.

A factor in favour of Britain was that early in October 1939, delegates of twenty-one American republics, meeting at Panama, had agreed that an American Security Zone should be declared of from three hundred to six hundred miles from their coasts. Churchill told President Roosevelt that Britain would observe the zone if the other belligerents did the same. Churchill wanted the United States Navy to patrol the zone and not some ineffectual neutral.

The *Graf Spee* had vanished again. She was well past Ascension Island and St Helena, with Langsdorff thinking in terms of further prizes.

Her day for a further conquest was 5th October, when, at 6.30 in the morning, smoke was spotted on the horizon. The ship was ordered to stop and a prize crew sent across. The vessel was identified as the 4,651-ton *Newton Beech*, registered at Newcastle upon Tyne and owned by the Tyneside Line. She was carrying maize.

This time there was to be no target practice with guns or torpedoes. For Langsdorff had decided that she should be used to accommodate crews from any other ships captured. The *Newton Beech* had sent out a signal, but this was weak and there seemed little chance that it would be picked up. The crew of the British vessel thought the Germans' behaviour rather unusual. They were not telling them to pack their belongings, but were examining the ship closely. It was then that the master, Captain J. Robison, learned that his ship was not to be sunk, but was to be used as a prison ship for the crews of other victims.

Like Captain Harris of the *Clement*, Captain Robison was taken aboard the *Graf Spee*, where he received orders to follow the *Graf Spee* in the *Newton Beech* under the watchful eyes of the prize crew. The bridge and the engine-room were well guarded. The Britishers realized that any attempt at overcoming the guards would be useless. The machine guns on the bridge would make short work of them. Even in the unlikely event of gaining control of the *Newton Beech*, it would not be long before the battleship would be in view and suspect that something was wrong.

Captain Robison decided there was little they could do, and that they would have to go along with the Germans, who were behaving strictly but correctly. He had at first been taken in by the fact that the battleship was flying a French flag until she had suddenly lowered this and run up the German flag in its place.

The *Graf Spee* was now searching in the area on the Freetown-Cape Town route. Langsdorff was hoping for more pickings. He was not to be disappointed. Early on the morning of Saturday, 7th October, a *Graf Spee* lookout spotted smoke on the horizon. Immediately, the pocket battleship swung into what had now become the accepted routine. Action stations was sounded, and a tingle of excitement ran through the ship.

The ship to which the *Graf Spee* was now making the usual signals of "Do not transmit" and "Heave to" was another British steamer, the 4,222-ton *Ashlea*, owned by the Cliffside Shipping Company and, like the *Newton Beech*, registered at Newcastle. She carried a cargo of sugar, and was to join a United Kingdom-bound convoy at Freetown.

When the master, Captain C. Pottinger, was told that a warship had been sighted, he at first thought, after observing her from the bridge, to which he had been called, that she was French. He saw no reason to stop, but when a signal was made not to transmit, he was in no doubt that the warship was anything but friendly.

Captain Pottinger had just time to destroy the confidential books before a boat was bumping alongside. The Germans came aboard and ranged over the *Ashlea*.

"You have ten minutes in which to leave your ship, Herr Kapitaen," a German officer told the *Ashlea*'s master. The crew of thirty-five packed what clothing and other personal possessions they could in the time available. While they were doing this, the German boarding party was taking the opportunity to replenish the *Graf Spee*'s sugar stocks by taking a quantity of sugar from the *Ashlea*'s cargo.

"Looks like the Germans have got a sweet tooth as well. I could do with a cuppa myself just now after this little lot," one man exclaimed as the crew lined up ready to leave the ship.

"Come on, lads, hurry it up," urged Captain Pottinger. They assembled on deck with their possessions and were preparing to leave when a shout went up. For in sight came the *Newton Beech*. "What's this, then?" said a voice among the *Ashlea*'s crew.

"That, gentlemen, is the ship to which you are being taken. Your ship is to be sunk," said the German officer.

"Poor old *Ashlea*. She's a gonner," muttered someone. But there was no time to mourn the fate of the ship. "Into the boats," came the order. The Germans were meanwhile laying cartridge charges. A neat, quick job was planned. The *Ashlea* died without fuss. There was no need for torpedoes or gunfire.

On board the *Newton Beech*, the newcomers from the *Ashlea* exchanged experiences and speculated on what was to happen to them. Unless by some chance the British Navy came upon them, it seemed to many that they must end up in a German prison camp.

Yet had they but known it, Langsdorff was having his own problems about taking captured ships with the *Graf Spee*. It was becoming apparent that putting prize crews on captured ships and having these ships in the vicinity was bound to cause problems. For one thing, there was the question of speed and for another the matter of fuel. They also posed another source of danger to the pocket battleship, creating more chances of being sighted.

If the *Graf Spee* arrived at her next meeting with the *Altmark* with a string of captured ships, then more difficulties would be made. There would be an even greater chance of detection. They had had two lucky escapes so far—with the British cruiser and the unknown ship—and to have several ships hove to in a limited area would greatly increase the chances of being seen. Having to put on board prize crews also depleted the crew of the *Graf Spee*.

Alone in his cabin, Langsdorff pondered this question. He could not put the *Graf Spee* at even more risk than she was already. Strike and disappear—that was the *Graf Spee*'s role. She must not be slowed down for any reason. The *Altmark* also needed to be free to disappear once she had refuelled the battleship. There was only one thing for it—the *Newton Beech*, now carrying the crew of the *Ashlea*, in addition to her own, must be sunk.

The order was given for the transfer of the crews of the *Newton Beech* and the *Ashlea*: "Into the boats." The crews followed the Germans' order. They scrambled aboard the *Graf Spee* and could not help but admire the smartness of the pocket battleship and the smart turnout of the crew.

Again, cartridge shells were to be the means of sending the *Newton Beech* to the bottom. The charges went off without incident, but the ship did not sink at once. It was to be several hours later before she sank because of her cargo of maize.

It was getting near the time for the *Graf Spee* to have another meeting with her supply ship, but before then the raider was to make another capture that was to prove indirectly of some benefit to the crews of the ships subsequently held prisoner in the *Altmark*. The latest capture occurred on 10th October after smoke had been sighted early in the evening by the *Graf Spee* lookouts. The sighting once more brought the usual flurry of activity. As binoculars were trained on the vessel, it could be seen that she was larger than those so far captured by the *Graf Spee*.

The ship was the 8,196-ton *Huntsman*, of Liverpool, with Captain A. Brown as master. She had a crew of eighty-four, including Indians, and was on passage to Freetown. Her cargo included carpets, jute and tea. It was this cargo that was to be the means of providing some degree of comfort for the captured British merchant seamen.

The large number of the crew of the freighter posed another problem for Langsdorff. The crews of the *Newton Beech* and *Ashlea* were already aboard the *Graf Spee* in what had been a crowded ship before the British were taken prisoner. So once more a British ship steamed in the wake of the raider, a prize crew on board, and keeping a watchful eye on their captives.

The crew of the *Huntsman* had no alternative but to submit. Resistance against the heavily armed Germans was out of the question. Captain Brown and his chief officer, A. Thompson, fully realized this and advised the crew to accept that there was nothing they could do, even if some of the younger ones felt inclined to hasty action. Even they, however, appreciated that they would be dead men if they were tempted to try anything. The Germans were polite but firm—and armed.

The date for a further rendezvous with the *Altmark* had been fixed for 14th October. Langsdorff decided that the *Graf Spee* must leave the *Huntsman* for the time being, meet the tanker and then return with her to the *Huntsman*.

The *Graf Spee* and the *Altmark* met on the morning of the 14th without incident. Dau, in company with Third Officer Schmidt, went aboard the battleship with a jaunty air, after seeing four British flags flying from the *Graf Spee*, trophies of her "kills". His joy was short-lived when Langsdorff told him that the prisoners from the *Graf Spee* and the crew of the *Huntsman* would have to be transferred to the *Altmark*.

Dau was going to object, but realized that to do so with this polite but firm German Navy officer was useless. The matter was settled as far as Langsdorff was concerned. He wanted the *Huntsman* sent to the bottom, too. This would then leave the *Graf Spee* free to continue her war on merchant shipping.

Dau was left with the problem of making arrangements to accommodate his unwelcome guests. There was only one advantage, and this was that there was more space available now that the *Graf Spee* had taken a large amount of stores carried in the tanker.

"We have to take the prisoners," Dau reported when he returned to the *Altmark*. "The *Spee* is crowded enough already with her own crew. Some of them were left behind in Germany because of lack of space," Dau commented.

"Dr Tyrolt, we must do what we can to see that the prisoners are treated according to the conditions of war. They are merchant seamen, but they are still prisoners-of-war. You will do the best you can with the supplies you have available if any of them become sick, or are sick when we take them aboard." Tyrolt just hoped that there would be no sickness among the prisoners.

Dau went on an inspection of the *Altmark*. The storerooms, he decided, could be turned into accommodation for the prisoners. They comprised four decks. The means of reaching the deck of the *Altmark* was by way of trunkways. These trunkways were secured on the main deck by hatchways, and were easily guarded in case of attempted breakouts. The guards from the *Graf Spee* would also stand no nonsense, Dau reasoned. They were young Germans brought up in the ways of modern Germany, not merchant seamen who had spent half their lives at sea and who had a comradely feeling for fellow seamen.

Weichert was to be the go-between in any matters concerning the captives. Dr Tyrolt would be responsible for their medical well-being.

Walter Schmidt had enough to do as third officer without worrying about the prisoners. The engineers were also busy in their department and knew that sooner or later the question of the overhaul of the engines would have to be considered if the *Altmark* were to remain in the South Atlantic until the cruise was over. Langsdorff proposed to continue raiding the commerce routes until January before making a breakout for Germany, though he knew the South Atlantic must be alive with ships of the Royal Navy. The sinking of the *Clement* had alerted the Admiralty, and the other captive ships must be listed as overdue.

When the transfer of the prisoners began, it was the first time the crew of the *Altmark* had seen the enemy, although the war had been on for weeks. It made a welcome change from the monotony of sailing around in the ocean waiting for a meeting with the pocket battleship. Third Officer Schmidt went to his cabin for a camera and joined other members of the crew in lining the rails of the tanker as the boats from the *Graf Spee* and the *Huntsman*, which they had now met, came alongside the tanker. Schmidt pointed his camera at the *Huntsman*, got her in focus and "captured" the ship on film. Others were doing the same, and also getting close-ups of groups of prisoners as they scrambled aboard. It made a welcome break for them, and they also felt they were sharing in the *Graf Spee*'s victories.

Carpets and jute taken from the *Huntsman* were also hauled aboard the *Altmark* for use by the prisoners. Vegetables, meat, eggs and tea were also salvaged from the *Huntsman*. Whatever the future held, both the Germans and the prisoners knew that a long, hard time lay ahead.

"Look, lads, it's a Norwegian," a merchant seaman shouted as they neared the *Altmark*. The tanker was still in her guise as the *Sogne*, painted yellow. It did not take them long, however, to realize that this was no Norwegian ship to which they were to be transferred, but another German flying a false flag. They had already been taken in by the *Graf Spee* masquerading as a French warship, and now they had for a brief moment thought of freedom in the shape of a Norwegian tanker.

The captives boarded the *Altmark* and looked around with interest. They saw a man with a goatee beard regarding them critically. "Knitty Whiskers," someone murmured, and from then on the austere Dau was known by this name to the captives.

"Now then, mi'lads, let's have you." Chief Officer Thompson, of the *Huntsman*, gave a hand to marshal his men. Walter Schmidt nodded approvingly as the Merchant Navy officer helped to speed up the embarkation. Thompson was not helping the Germans, but wanted to make things easier for his own men. The crews of the *Newton Beech*, *Ashlea* and *Huntsman* were now aboard the tanker.

Third Officer Schmidt was impressed by the orderly manner in which the prisoners came aboard. Thompson's leadership was also helping. There were no problems as the captives prepared to make the best of things. The wisdom of bringing the carpets from the *Huntsman* was now becoming obvious as they were laid on the steel plating. The carpets provided some measure of comfort, and later were to provide warmth as the *Altmark* sailed deep into the cold wastes of the South Atlantic.

With suitcases, bags and clothing strewn about, the "flats" had a chaotic air as the prisoners stepped over each other and tried to stow their belongings. The only illumination was the electric light that streamed down. But with the adaptability of seamen everywhere, the captives did not take long to make themselves as comfortable as they could in the spartan conditions. The officers had their own quarters, and there was also separate accommodation for the Indians.

Dr Tyrolt had examined them, finding one man, a wireless operator, wounded, and a seaman suffering with a severe fever. He was to take care of both in the coming weeks and help them back to health. He found nothing seriously wrong with the others, though he thought they looked a motley lot in their old clothes, vests and torn shirts. They had had to take what they could when leaving their ships.

There now remained the question of the disposal of the *Huntsman*. This ship also proved to be one to die the hard way. The *Graf Spee* tried to sink her, and before nightfall the sea-valves of the *Huntsman* were destroyed, but still she did not sink. She took more than twelve hours to do so. Third Officer Schmidt felt a twinge of sympathy for Captain Brown as the master of the *Huntsman* stood at the rail of the *Altmark* and watched his ship in her final agony. "She was a good ship," he murmured simply as he turned from the rail.

The taking on board of the prisoners threw a strain on the *Altmark*'s food supplies. Dau had been looking forward to a meeting with a cargo ship carrying fresh food, especially vegetables, potatoes and eggs, at that time. The ship was to have sailed from Brazil and met the *Altmark* in the middle of the South Atlantic, but Dau received a message that the ship was being shadowed to the rendezvous position by a British submarine, with the object of destroying the *Altmark*.

"We cannot meet this ship," Dau told Paulsen. "It is too much of a risk." He ordered a change of course, and the rations were cut again. In spite of this setback, however, rations were adequate, even if there was little variation.

The *Graf Spee* had meanwhile claimed another victim as she swept another area off St Helena. On 22nd October the *Graf Spee*'s aircraft spotted the *Trevanion*, a steamer of more than 5,000 tons, owned by the Hain Steamship Company, of London. Her master was Captain J. N. Edwards, and she was homeward bound from Port Pirie, Australia, carrying a cargo of concentrates.

Langsdorff was again using the ruse of the French flag. The customary "Heave to" signal was sent. Captain Edwards ordered his radio operator, N. C. Martinson, to send an R.R.R. report. As he did so, the radio shack and upper deck were sprayed with machine-gun bullets.

Luckily, none of the crew was wounded. The Germans came aboard, the crew were given a few minutes to gather personal belongings, and preparations made to sink the ship. It was all over in less than two hours.

The *Graf Spee* met the *Altmark* on 28th October and transferred the *Trevanion*'s crew to the tanker, where the arrival of the newcomers caused a flutter of excitement among the other prisoners, now settling down to a routine.

The *Graf Spee* took on more fuel before making her departure after Dau had again met Langsdorff and been informed of future plans. The *Graf Spee* was off on what was to be a feint. Langsdorff planned a sortie in the Indian Ocean. A strike there would help convince the British that two raiders and not one were operating.

The hunting groups had already ranged widely without success. Langsdorff knew that an appearance in the Indian Ocean would create even more alarm. He entered the Indian Ocean early in November. His one and only victim in the Indian Ocean was a small steamer, the 706-ton *Africa Shell*, with a crew of twenty-nine and Captain Patrick Dove as master, which she caught in the Mozambique Channel on 15th November. The captain protested that they were inside Portuguese territorial waters, but this did not save the *Africa Shell*. The crew were allowed to take to the boats and head for the shore. Captain Dove was taken aboard the *Graf Spee*, and charges placed in the *Africa Shell*.

The *Graf Spee* slipped back into the Atlantic on 20th November. The hunting groups scoured far and wide without success. The fox had eluded the hunt. But was there one fox—or two?

3

My Apologies, Gentlemen

The third officer of the 10,441-ton refrigerated vessel *Doric Star*, William Melville-Evans, was having lunch as the Blue Star Line ship ploughed her way through the South Atlantic to Freetown, on Saturday, 2nd December. She had taken on dairy produce at Auckland, New Zealand, and a deck cargo of wool at Sydney. While at Auckland, a 4.7-inch gun had been fitted. Fuel had been taken on at Cape Town, and now all seemed set fair for Freetown, where she was to join a convoy for the United Kingdom.

It was just five minutes past one o'clock, ship's time, when, as the young Welsh third officer put another forkful of food to his mouth, there was a terrific explosion. "What the blazes is that?" he exclaimed, dropping his fork and rushing to his cabin for his steel helmet. As gunnery officer, it was his job to see that the gun was manned in an emergency, and this seemed like one. Some impulse also made him snatch up his camera while grabbing his helmet.

What Melville-Evans did not realize was that the *Doric Star* had been sighted by the *Graf Spee*, now hunting again after meeting the *Altmark* on 26th November and taking on fuel and supplies. A number of the prisoners—captains and officers—had also been transferred from the *Altmark* to the *Graf Spee*. Langsdorff had ordered the warning shot to be fired and the "Heave to" signal made. The *Doric Star* officers had now recovered from their surprise and Captain W. Stubbs ordered wireless operator William Comber to send out an R.R.R. report—"being attacked by surface raider". Another warning shot was fired by the *Graf Spee*, but the report went out.

While all this was going on, Melville-Evans had mustered his gun crew, who at first thought the attacker was a submarine. The raider was now in sight, but Melville-Evans was still undaunted. He was lining up on the target when Chief Officer Stanley Ranson shouted urgently over the phone: "For God's sake don't fire at that thing—it's a German battleship!" Nevertheless, Melville-Evans and his team kept the raider in the sights of their solitary "pop-gun", an old Japanese First World War weapon.

The third officer now found a use for his camera. He took photographs of the *Graf Spee*, which had everything pointed at the *Doric Star*, including torpedo tubes, 11-inch guns, 6-inch guns and machine-guns.

"For us with our solitary gun, it was just like showing a pop-gun to a robber with a big revolver," he was to recall later.

Ranson, realizing the hopelessness of the situation, told the gun crew to dump the breech overboard. Reluctantly, Melville-Evans also threw overboard the camera containing what would have been historic film, as Captain Stubbs thought the Germans would confiscate it. It occurred to the third officer later that he could easily have removed the film and kept it hidden among his possessions.

The German boarding party were now heading for the *Doric Star*, but before they arrived the *Doric Star*'s officers collected navigating equipment and charts. The charts they rolled up and carried under their arms. By chance, Melville-Evans, who had taken a magnetic variation chart of the Atlantic, did not roll his up. He folded it into squares and pushed it inside his shirt. His motive was not concealment, but merely to protect it from spray and dirt while being taken across to the raider. Yet that simple act was to have important repercussions. For though the Germans removed the charts from the other officers, they overlooked the one carried by Melville-Evans. It was to play an important role in subsequent events.

Archibald Willis, the second mate, who was something of an artist and could turn out lightning sketches to entertain his fellow officers, managed to take a few crayons and pencils with him.

Willis had had a grandstand view of events. He was on watch when the first explosion occurred, and had sounded the alarm. Now he waited with the others as the *Graf Spee* launch came alongside. The *Doric Star*'s boats had already been lowered into the water. Water was flooding into the engine room, for the captain had given the order for the sea-valves to be opened.

The Germans clambered on board and at once gave orders that the ship must be cleared in ten minutes. Suitcases and clothing were hurriedly scrambled together. The officers almost looked as if they were gathering for a conference as they stood around clutching charts, sextants and other navigating equipment.

The *Graf Spee* had been disguised again, and was now bearing the name *Deutschland* on her stern. The *Doric Star* was her best prize so far, but the Blue Star ship was also to be the means of bringing the British Navy on Langsdorff's heels.

Now, however, there was the pressing problem of the *Doric Star*. Her crew were aboard the pocket battleship, but the *Doric Star* was no longer seaworthy and must be disposed of. Guns and a torpedo, in addition to scuttling charges, were used to send her to the bottom. It was a sad end for the *Doric Star*, which had been built by Lithgow's of Port Glasgow, and had started her life with voyages to China and Japan.

For the latest captives of the *Graf Spee*, there was no time to mourn the passing of their ship. Melville-Evans, who had been at sea since he was fifteen and was now twenty-two, had seen nothing like the *Graf Spee*. He had sailed the world in freighters and had experienced conditions as rough as any of those undergone by members of the seafaring families from which he was descended. None had ever been aboard such a ship as he now found himself. He was impressed by the immaculate appearance of both ship and crew.

"A beautiful ship," he commented to Willis as the Germans ushered them below decks. He was also now aware that the ship was the *Graf Spee*. The disguise was only for observation at long range.

The Germans were taking no chances with their captives. First they had to strip completely and to bundle their clothes up, which the Germans allowed them to do themselves. But they did not search them at that time. The clothes were put into a fumigating tank, and guards, with bayonets fixed, stood by watchfully as liberal use was made of soap and disinfectant. The Germans were not going to run the risk of any disease from the British seamen, who were then allowed to dress and given a meal.

It soon became apparent that the Germans were living in over-crowded conditions. There were men sleeping in hammocks in every alleyway. The hammocks were taken down after use and slung up neatly. All the time, sailors were passing along the alleyways, pushing past each other. Cramped for space they might have been, but Melville-Evans had to admire the typical German thoroughness with which the crew coped with the conditions.

He himself would have welcomed one of the hammocks, for he had spent the night in the lavatory, trying to sleep. He was compelled to find what rest he could perched on the lavatory seat, but was constantly disturbed as men pushed in to use the lavatory.

It was 5.30 on the Sunday morning and Melville-Evans had just fallen into another fitful doze when he was jerked awake by the crash of the "action" alarm. The *Graf Spee* had sighted another victim—the 7,983-ton *Tairoa*, a cargo vessel of the Shaw Saville and Albion Company. She had taken on meat, butter and wool around the Australian coast and had left Melbourne on 3rd November for the United Kingdom, by way of South Africa.

Fifteen days later, when some three days out from Durban, Captain William Starr, master of the *Tairoa*, received the news of the sinking of the *Africa Shell*, a few hundred miles north of Durban by a German raider.

"I don't like this at all, gentlemen. In fact, I'm damn worried," said Captain Starr to his officers as they discussed the news. The *Tairoa* coaled at Durban, which she left on Sunday, 23rd November. Passing down the African coast, they were "visited" by British bombers and also saw one or two cruisers which made the *Tairoa*'s crew feel more cheerful and hopeful of reaching Freetown to pick up a convoy for the United Kingdom. Their cheerfulness was short-lived, however, as on Saturday, 2nd December, at around midday they heard the R.R.R. signal from the *Doric Star*. The Blue Star Line ship was then about 180 miles north of the *Tairoa*'s position.

"Keep a sharp lookout," ordered Captain Starr, who had a feeling that it would not be long before they received attention from the raider. His forebodings were realized when, early the following morning, the navigating officers spotted a ship. Soon they identified her as a large warship of unknown nationality bearing down on them at around thirty knots. Now she was near enough for them to make out the Swastika.

"It's the raider," exclaimed Starr as the "Heave to, do not transmit" signal was made. But the radio officer, Cummins, had already started to transmit. That was too much for Langsdorff, and the *Graf Spee* opened fire. The shells blasted into the bridge and radio cabin until the wireless equipment was shot away and transmission ceased. Only then did Cummins give up. It was a brave effort.

Most of the *Tairoa*'s company were now in the boats, abandoning the ship, which had been badly damaged on her upperworks by the gunfire. The battleship had moved to within two hundred yards, and a boarding party was on the way. The Germans came alongside and ordered the crew back on board.

W. F. (Wally) Wells, seventh engineer of the *Tairoa*, struggled back on board with his belongings and wondered what the Germans had in store for them. He joined the others as they were mustered by the German officer in charge. He told them that the *Tairoa* was to follow the pocket battleship as a store ship for a few days.

That was the idea, but it was found that the steering gear had been shot from the bridge. When this was reported to the Germans, along with the fact that the *Tairoa* was not capable of any more than 12 knots, Captain Starr was told that he and his crew would be taken aboard the pocket battleship and his vessel sunk. The crew were given a few minutes in which to collect eating utensils and other belongings before they were all mustered again to board the raider's motor launch for transfer to the *Graf Spee*.

"Look," said Wally Wells, as the launch drew near to the raider, "it's the *Deutschland*." Then they noticed that one funnel and one gun turret were made from canvas and poles. But as they went aboard they realized it was all camouflage and that the raider was actually the *Graf Spee*.

Like the crew of the *Doric Star*, the *Tairoa* crew were given a thorough medical examination. Once more the Germans were taking no chances of any disease being introduced by captives. At least there was some satisfaction for the crew of the *Tairoa* in that the examination was followed by a dish of thick soup and coffee, even though the coffee was cold.

Once the captives were imprisoned below decks, there came the business of sinking the *Tairoa*, which was done by shell and torpedo. The sea was disturbed for a time and then there was nothing to mark her passing except for flotsam. "That's the end of the old ship," a man commented as they felt the *Graf Spee* moving off at high speed in a westerly direction.

With their ships gone, the *Doric Star* and *Tairoa* crews had nothing else to do but to compare notes, make the most of their cramped conditions and watch the Germans go about their duties. Wally Wells found that in spite of himself he was impressed by the *Graf Spee*'s crew. He had to admit that both officers and men were trying to give them as good a time as circumstances permitted. "Not a bad bunch," he thought.

Then, on that Sunday afternoon, with the sun blazing down, the crews of both the *Doric Star* and the *Tairoa* was mustered on deck. There, on the spotless deck, with the South Atlantic Ocean for a backcloth, the captives were given a treat. A marine band was playing, with awnings providing shelter from the hot sun. The spotless white decks gleamed.

"Just like Sunday afternoon at home," quipped a member of the *Doric Star* crew. "Only needs the wife to make it like a treat out to the town park with the band playing." Archibald Willis thought that the scene would make a good subject for sketching if he had been allowed. Melville-Evans thought he had seen nothing like it in all his days at sea.

Suddenly they saw him—Kapitaen zur See Langsdorff, the man who was leading the British Navy a dance; the man who had so far sunk eight ships without loss of life. Now here he was playing host to the crews of captured British merchant ships. "My apologies, gentlemen. It is the fortunes of war," said Langsdorff, smartly clad in white uniform, as he moved among the captives. "Please make yourself as comfortable as possible."

The prisoners had earlier discovered that the ship was equipped with a laundry run by Chinese, and now there was a band playing. It seemed incredible to the British, more accustomed to the rough and ready life of a freighter. It seemed more as if the *Graf Spee* was on a "showing the flag" cruise than engaged in the deadly business of war on commerce.

Langsdorff was in affable mood. The captives also found his second in command, Kapitaen zur See Kay, a decent sort. It seemed that the Germans were determined to do what they could for their prisoners. Meanwhile, the prisoners themselves made the best of the chance to relax. Things might be different in a few days.

They were indeed to find things different within a few days. The raider was to meet the *Altmark* on the Wednesday, 6th December. At noon on that day, the *Graf Spee* came up with the *Altmark*, still sailing under the name of *Sogne*. For a moment, the prisoners, like the others before them, were mystified by the Norwegian registration. There were some who thought it was a neutral, but quickly realized that this modern tanker was the vessel that was supplying the *Graf Spee*.

Once again, the sea surrounding the two vessels was alive with activity as the prisoners were transferred and Dau made his usual visit to confer with Langsdorff. "More prisoners!" he thought. He was aghast, but did not dare protest to Langsdorff, who had more important things on his mind. The battleship was now beginning to show signs of her months at sea and needed overhaul. Arrangements were made for another meeting place. The following morning the ships parted, and sailed out of each other's lives. For they were destined never to meet again.

Some British officers were kept on board the *Graf Spee*, but the bulk of the captives was transferred to the *Altmark*. There the newcomers were given a warm welcome by the prisoners already in the tanker and anxious for the latest news. They swept aside the guards and Weichert and Lieutenant Schmidt. "Babyface" Schmidt and Weichert were important links between the prisoners and the Germans.

The new influx of prisoners meant more problems for the crew of the *Altmark*. Schwill, the cook, and Treibel, the baker, had the important task of seeing to the preparations of the rations, as allocated by Dau.

The new prisoners were finding the atmosphere of the *Altmark* in stark contrast to that of the *Graf Spee*. They had been mustered by the guards, who were armed with dirks and revolvers, and searched for matches and torches and for any other means of making a light.

Melville-Evans found himself in the top flat with the other officers. The flat was about 60 feet by 45 feet and 7 feet high. He saw there were two small trunkways, one at either end, leading up to the deck. In one of them was a primitive lavatory made from an empty five-gallon paint drum with the top sawn off. Two rough plank tables were in the centre of the flat, which accommodated 55 officers.

Those first few hours were bedlam as the prisoners settled down among those who had already made something of a home in the flats. Melville-Evans and Wally Wells struggled with carpets taken from the cargo of the *Huntsman* and put them on the floor. They stretched out on the carpets, then found that once everyone was lying on the deck there was hardly room to turn over without digging someone in the ribs. They stored their belongings where they could and tried to rest. So began their first day of captivity in the *Altmark*.

The second deck served as a washroom. The prisoners were issued with a daily quart of water, in which they had to wash, stripping off and bathing the best way they could. After that, they swilled out a towel or small article of clothing, since water and soap—one tablet had to last six weeks—were so short. An extra quart of water was issued every sixth day for washing clothing. Whether the clothes were washed or not, depended on whether soap was available. Most prisoners wore as little as possible, while those who had been lucky enough to bring a pair of khaki shorts were better off than those who had to make do with trousers. In the flats, with their lack of proper ventilation and light, most were stripped to the waist and wore neither shoes nor socks.

Because of the shortage of water, the prisoners were allowed to wash only once a day. This was a real deprivation for the weather was warm. Melville-Evans mused on the luxury of a cooling shower or bath. He had seen little on this first day to make him think that he was going to enjoy his time in the *Altmark*.

The conditions were not too good in the top flat occupied by the officers, but they were more fortunate than the members of their crews who were accommodated in the two decks below the deck that served as a washroom. One deck was a smoke-room where the prisoners could smoke, if they had any tobacco or cigarettes or could scrounge some. Matches were supplied at the rate of one box every second day.

The Indian crew, or Lascars, from the *Huntsman* had separate accommodation, and the remaining sixty or so white members of crews were confined in the after end of the *Altmark*.

The newcomers were introduced to what one wag termed "Hotel Altmark". There were set times for meals, if such they could be called. The time-table was: Breakfast 7 a.m. Three slices of rye bread and butter with tea without sugar or milk. Lunch 12 noon: Soup every day. Rice or macaroni three times a week. Tinned fruit twice a week. Beetroot once a week. Tea 4.30 p.m.: Three slices of bread and butter with cheese, a small portion of sausage or tinned meat. A pint of tea. (Meat, it turned out, was served twice in three months.)

Two men from each flat went to the galley each day for the food, served it and then did the washing up. The officers' flat was divided into two messes, one of thirty and the other of twenty-five, so that each man had a turn at the chores every twelve days.

It was generally agreed that the food was wholesome, but there was not enough of it. Many hours were to be spent later talking of meals they had enjoyed in the past and of those they hoped to enjoy in the future.

"Well," said Melville-Evans, "the food might not be much, but at least it's no worse than that I had as an apprentice, and some of the conditions we lived in then. . . . I remember we were anchored off Houston once, which was swampy in those days, when the biggest mosquitoes I have ever seen swarmed into our cabin. We were using oil lamps, because they shut the power right down, which made it even more warm than it was. They swarmed down on us. They had yellow and black stripes like football jerseys. One chap had 150 bites."

"No; I've seen worse," said the *Doric Star*'s third mate as he regaled his companions in the flat with some of his experiences.

He found himself thinking at odd moments of his early life at sea and of his upbringing in Wales, where he had been born twenty-two years earlier. His father had started his working life as a butcher before opening shops in several Welsh ports and becoming a ships' chandler. He also had several farms until his business and farms became victims of the Depression like so many other enterprises.

So his son had gone to sea at the age of fifteen at the height of the Depression, and considered himself lucky to get a position at all. He had experienced all the joys and fears of a young boy at sea and recalled that on one voyage they had been issued with lime juice, the old-time seaman's protection against scurvy. They had been on such a low-vitamin diet and eating salt beef after the vegetables and fresh meat supplies had been exhausted that lime juice was essential.

His first voyage had been one of four years and three months. He smiled as he thought of his father's first words as they met after such a long absence: "Hello, son. You haven't grown much, have you?" He had replied: "I haven't grown at all." He had thought that the diet might have had something to do with it. At least it was not any worse in the *Altmark*, he reflected as he drank a mug of tea, part of the cargo salvaged from the *Huntsman*. "Thank God we can have a mug of tea, even if there is no milk," he exclaimed among the general conversation as they lingered over the evening meal before settling down for the night.

On that first day the newcomers had been allowed the ninety minutes' exercise period on deck under guard. It had given them the opportunity to examine the *Altmark*, or *Sogne* as she was still named, at closer quarters. The supply ship was alone now that the *Graf Spee* had gone her way. They saw Dau and his officers watching them from the bridge. They saw him make some remark and point. Obviously something about the prisoners had caught his eye. He looked stern as he gazed down at them.

Below, each day they were visited at 10 a.m. by "Babyface" Schmidt and Dr Tyrolt, who made an inspection. Tyrolt was disposed to be friendly, while Schmidt, who was only twenty-two, was inclined to be stiff and formal at first, but was to unbend later as he came to know the prisoners. The well-travelled doctor was soon chatting away, and the prisoners got to know something of his background. He had been to university and had done many jobs. A great deal of his life had been spent in America.

His efforts to speak English amused the prisoners, and they laughed at his expense, but he wanted to learn as much English as possible and did not mind them making fun of him. It was this attitude that was later to win him admiration and respect from the captives. He had few medical supplies and his cure-all was for his patients to drink salt water.

"I wonder what the old man's like?" asked one of the newcomers in the officers' flat. "A Nazi," someone replied. They had not long to wait. On the second day of the newcomers' arrival in the *Altmark*, all the prisoners were mustered on deck under the eyes of twelve armed guards, who, in addition to rifles, carried hand grenades.

Then Dau (or Knitty Whiskers as they called him behind his back) strode out and began to address them. "England," he said, thrusting out his chin, "will not win this war she has made to try to reduce Germany to a slave state. We have not yet any colonies to put you on, but soon we will have." He bristled with rage as his outburst was greeted with laughter.

He went on to describe what he called the bad treatment some German prisoners were receiving at the hands of the British. "But we will treat you according to the rules of war," he told the men dressed in singlets, dirty trousers and tattered shirts. The weather was warm and they were at least in the open air. Even listening to Dau was better than being cooped up in the flats.

"The Navy will get us out of this. They'll have the *Spee* and then search for us. They must know we are prisoners. The raider reports must have been picked up by now," said one officer as they settled down in the flat that night.

Wally Wells and Melville-Evans were inclined to agree. Getting out those reports had been brave actions on the part of the radio operators, and could easily have led to them being killed.

It was only one day after leaving the *Altmark* that the *Graf Spee* made what was to prove to be her final kill. The last victim was the 3,895-ton *Streonshalh*, whose smoke was spotted early in the evening as she plodded towards Freetown to join a convoy. The vessel, registered at Whitby, Yorkshire, had a crew of thirty-two and a cargo of wheat. Her master was Captain J. Robinson and she had been on her way from Montevideo when intercepted by the *Graf Spee*. The crew were taken aboard the battleship and the ship sunk. Langsdorff could hardly be pleased with so small a prize on the River Plate route with its well-laden ships plying from South America.

The addition of Captain Robinson and his crew to the number of prisoners—officers and captains—that Langsdorff had decided should remain in the *Graf Spee* did nothing to help the problem of space. The transfer of most of the captives to the *Altmark* had helped to improve matters, but there was no room to spare. There was consolation, however, in that the newcomers made a break in routine for the prisoners already in the *Graf Spee* and there was plenty to talk about. Captain Robinson and his men learned of the *Altmark* and of the British seamen she was carrying in her holds.

"Her captain's a real Tartar. Proper Nazi," Captain Robinson was told. "We'll no doubt be meeting up with her again when the raider is ready for more supplies. Can't say I'm anxious to see her again." Others agreed. They were among those officers transferred from the *Altmark* to the *Graf Spee*. Langsdorff, for his part, had arranged another rendezvous with his supply ship, but first he planned to plunder along the River Plate route.

In the *Altmark*, Dau was busy with his new charges and preening himself on the *Graf Spee*'s victories. "We are doing well," he told Paulsen. "We shall meet the *Graf Spee* after she has struck at more ships. The British are fond of hunting, but they will find the *Graf Spee* a wily fox. Langsdorff is a fine sailor and the *Graf Spee* a fine ship. We must be ready for when the cruise is over and we can begin the run for Germany."

Not a few of the crew would have been willing to start the run for Germany at any time. They had not been ashore since August and were tired of the never-ending sight of the ocean. Even the warmth of the sun was proving poor compensation. There was little change in the diet, too, despite the best efforts of Schwill, the cook, and the baker, Treibel.

The problem of fresh water and food was worrying for Dau. He thought it was all right for Langsdorff to sink ships, but now it had been found impossible to keep any as prizes it was possible that the *Altmark* would have to accommodate more prisoners before the voyage home began. If, however, the *Graf Spee* sank any ships within sight of the coast, Langsdorff would let the crews head for the shore. It was certain that, being the man he was, he would not leave them to the mercy of the sea.

Dr Tyrolt was also concerned from the health point of view. His inspection of the British and the Indians had given him little cause for concern. He was aware that if serious disease did occur among them he had little hope of containing it alone. The primitive sanitary arrangements would not help. The waste was simply tipped overboard each day by the same men who took the food to their fellow prisoners.

All was well at the moment, though, and the Germans wondered how the *Graf Spee* was progressing. None realized it then, but time was running out for Langsdorff and the pocket battleship. The fateful 13th of December was drawing near. The hunted and the hunters were drawing closer together. The hunting forces of the British Navy had not been idle.

A hunch played by Commodore Henry Harwood, who commanded the South America Division of the South Atlantic Squadron, was about to pay off. The scene was set for what was to become the Battle of the River Plate.

4

The End of the *Graf Spee*

Sailors are generally regarded as being superstitious, but few of those in the *Graf Spee* and the *Altmark* had any reason to think that 13th December 1939 would turn out to be a day of misfortune. The day began like so many others in that region, holding all the promise of being warm and sunny. There was a light swell and a moderate breeze. Visibility, as the sun came up, had increased to twenty miles.

The *Graf Spee* lookouts were keeping their customary alert watch. Would another unsuspecting British cargo ship fall into their hands today as she plodded along the rich shipping routes of the Plate area? Langsdorff and his officers were anxious for a really good "kill" before the pocket battleship bid farewell to the South Atlantic and set course for Germany. Nine ships had been sunk, but more important she had spread anxiety in the South Atlantic and the Indian Ocean as well as pinning down British Naval forces. All this had been done without loss of life, and Langsdorff had some cause to be pleased with himself. But another prize would not be amiss.

It was then that the day's events were set in motion. A lookout sighted two tiny masts, and almost immediately afterwards four more masts were observed. The *Graf Spee*'s crew were soon closed up at action stations.

It was at that moment that things started to go wrong for Langsdorff. In truth, however, his luck had started to run out on 2nd December, when the *Doric Star* had got off her R.R.R. signal. This had been picked up, and as a result British Naval forces were alerted as to the position at that time of the raider. Commodore Harwood had made a shrewd guess that Langsdorff would make for the Plate area. It was there that he would find the prizes that he sought. Commodore Harwood even calculated that the *Graf Spee* would reach the area by 13th December. The guess had proved right, and now Langsdorff was to pay dearly.

Langsdorff made a fatal error in the first vital minutes of the sighting of the masts. One lot were identified as belonging to the cruiser *Exeter*, armed with six 8-inch guns. The other ships, it was decided, were destroyers and that the three warships were guarding a convoy that must be below the horizon.

Langsdorff had been too eager. The other ships were not destroyers, but the 6-inch gun cruisers *Ajax* and *Achilles*, part of Force G covering the east coast of South America. The other member of the force, the 8-inch gun cruiser *Cumberland* was refitting in the Falkland Islands. With battle ensigns flying, the German pocket battleship and the British cruisers surged forward for the fateful encounter.

Langsdorff had the advantage of the *Graf Spee*'s 11-inch guns, with their greater weight and range. The British cruisers were handicapped in that they had not this power, but if they got close enough they could inflict a blow that could prove fatal in the circumstances. Where does a lone raider go for repairs? These were no harmless British merchant ships the *Graf Spee* was meeting—the Royal Navy had arrived to square accounts.

It was 6.17 a.m. when the *Graf Spee* opened fire, the *Exeter* being selected as the first target. Shells began to fall around her. Then it was the turn of the *Ajax*, from which Commodore Harwood was commanding the action, to receive attention from the *Graf Spee* and great splashes of water were thrown up. The *Exeter* was blazing away at the *Graf Spee*, and the *Achilles*, of the New Zealand Division of the Royal Navy, joined in.

Meanwhile, Commodore Harwood had had an enemy sighted report sent. This would bring the pack hurrying to the quarry, now fighting for her life but handing out heavy punishment in the process.

The *Exeter* was taking a severe hammering, B turret being knocked out and all the communications on the bridge being destroyed. Most of those on the bridge were cut down by splinters. It was a scene of carnage as Captain F. S. Bell, who had miraculously survived, and those on the bridge still remaining alive continued as best they could with communications wrecked. There was nothing for it but to steer the ship from aft, using messengers. The *Graf Spee*'s shells kept thundering into the *Exeter*, until the gallant cruiser, without power supply and her remaining guns useless, had to withdraw from the action.

Langsdorff tried to confuse the enemy by making smoke, but he could not shake off the *Ajax* and *Achilles*. Both cruisers were damaged, the two after turrets in the *Ajax* being knocked out. Both ships were still in fighting order and hitting the *Graf Spee*. The *Exeter* had also hit the *Graf Spee* before having to break off the action. A "chink" in the armour of the *Graf Spee* was found when a shell slammed into the galley and another in the bakery. Some damage was also done to the electric supply that powered shell hoists.

Shells continued to fall on the raider, and then Commodore Harwood came to the decision to break off the fight until nightfall—the battle had then been in progress for an hour and twenty minutes. Langsdorff decided that the *Graf Spee* was in no fit state to make a break for Germany. His ship must have her damage repaired, and for this she must go into port. But which? It was decided that Montevideo would be the best choice in the circumstances. The *Graf Spee*, with her dead and wounded, made for port, *Ajax* and *Achilles* tailing her.

All this time, the British officers held captive in the *Graf Spee* had been living in a nightmare of their own. The first explosions had roused them to a state of anxious alertness. They could see very little through the hole in the door. All knew that a shell landing in the right place—or wrong place, depending on how you looked at it—would mean the end for them, or at best leave them seriously wounded. A shell landing in a confined space was something they preferred not to think about. They could see bodies being piled up and hear the cries of the wounded. The *Graf Spee* was a beautiful ship—or was until the fighting began—but this was what she was built for; she might look regal in "showing the flag" exercises in peacetime, but this was her real destiny—to slay or to be slain. The beauty was now looking ravaged.

The *Graf Spee* arrived in Montevideo, while the *Ajax* and *Achilles* kept watch outside ready to pounce if she should decide to make a break for it. British and German signals began to flow back and forth as each side considered the latest development. Winston Churchill, as First Lord of the Admiralty, had been a close observer of the battle from the Admiralty War Room. Orders were sent out to the scattered hunting groups to converge on Montevideo. The fox was now in the lair and was not to be allowed to escape.

Thus began a game of bluff. It was essential to give the impression that should the *Graf Spee* break out she would have more to contend with than two British cruisers, already mauled in the battle. British Naval units, including the *Ark Royal* and *Renown*, were days away, though the *Cumberland* was making all speed from the Falkland Islands. The *Ajax* and *Achilles* were alone until the arrival of the *Cumberland* on the night of 14th December. The Germans were under the impression that reinforcements had arrived or were not far off.

Langsdorff was in constant touch with the German Admiralty. He pointed out that a breakout was not possible, and asked whether he should scuttle his ship or opt for internment. The reply instructed him to extend the time he was allowed in neutral waters, and to fight his way through to Buenos Aires if possible. There was to be no internment in Uruguay, but in the case of scuttling every effort was to be made to destroy the *Graf Spee* effectively.

The Uruguayan Government had granted seventy-two hours in addition to the twenty-four the pocket battleship had spent in port, and despite the fact that under international law a belligerent warship was not allowed to stay more than twenty-four hours in the territorial waters of a neutral power. Under international law, too, if a merchant ship of a belligerent nation sailed from a neutral port, a warship of the other country was not allowed to sail for twenty-four hours.

As the behind-the-scenes activity was engaged in by both sides, the British Merchant Navy officers released from the *Graf Spee* had a unique place in the episode. They had been taken prisoner, seen their ships sunk, lived through the *Graf Spee*'s engagement with the British cruisers and now they were honouring the German dead. They attended the funeral of the thirty-six Germans killed in the battle and placed a wreath on the coffins. The simple tribute read: "To the memory of brave men of the sea from their comrades of the British Merchant Service."

The British sailed a merchant ship, which meant a twenty-four hour delay for the *Graf Spee*. Everything was conspiring against Langsdorff. Even the damage to the galley would mean inconvenience in the feeding of the crew. Langsdorff considered all the points and came to what he considered in the circumstances the right decision—to scuttle.

Meanwhile, Montevideo had taken on a festive air. Thousands were gathered waiting for the next move, while the world's Press and radio correspondents flocked there. The talk in the bars and cafés was all about what Langsdorff would do. Some of them had seen this lonely figure as he attended the funeral of the *Graf Spee* dead. They had noticed that the responsibility and worry had taken their toll. Sympathy they might feel for Langsdorff as a man, but the people were caught up in the fever of the occasion. Would the Germans fight? What were the British doing? The questions were asked in the bars, which were enjoying brisk business. People were jockeying for the best positions to see the next move in the drama.

Correspondents reported every fact they could glean, and when they could not get facts they resorted to conjecture. This was a "big story" and the journalists were making the most of it. It was a Roman holiday for Montevideo. It was easy to forget that in a few hours men might die in their scores or be horribly maimed by flying splinters of red-hot metal. The war between Great Britain and Germany was at Montevideo's front door, and the people were going to see it at first hand while they could.

Langsdorff, once having decided to scuttle, thought of his men. Plans were made to take them off the *Graf Spee*, and also for them to go to Buenos Aires. The scene was set for the last act on this day, Sunday, 17th December.

Langsdorff had told the German Ambassador in Montevideo, Dr Otto Langmann, in a letter, of his intention to scuttle. The time limit placed on the *Graf Spee* by the Uruguayan authorities expired at 2000 hours. This was regardless of whether or not the repairs were completed. Most of the *Graf Spee*'s crew would be taken on board the German ship *Tacoma* in the harbour. Some 700 men were accordingly transferred, leaving only the scuttling party on board the *Graf Spee*.

The crowds suddenly ceased their chatter and all eyes were on the *Graf Spee* as the pocket battleship slipped her moorings at 6.15 p.m. The *Tacoma* followed shortly afterwards. The last stages of the drama were about to be played out. Many wondered if the *Graf Spee* would fight. Waiting outside, the British wondered the same thing. They were tense, but ready to settle the issue one way or the other. Three small vessels were on hand to take off the remaining members of the *Graf Spee*'s crew.

The end came at six minutes to nine o'clock. The night sky was torn apart by a great explosion as the *Graf Spee* ended her days in an orgy of flame and blast. It hardly needed the *Ajax*'s aircraft to report: "*Graf Spee* has blown herself up."

The speculation was over. The raider that the Royal Navy had hunted for so long was now just a mass of twisted, smouldering metal. The crowds gazed in awe as this once graceful fighting machine writhed in her death throes like some prehistoric monster gasping its last in the slime.

It was a bleak moment for Langsdorff, his crew and the German diplomats who had tried so hard to help Langsdorff. Now the crowds who had waited expectantly these last few days were seeing at first hand that the Third Reich was not invincible. The British had waited outside—still without the *Renown* and *Ark Royal*—and were prepared to fight it out, but Langsdorff had refused the encounter. He made the initial mistake of thinking the British warships he had seen on 13th December were screening a convoy, and had stirred up a hornets' nest. Now, with his decision to scuttle, he had left himself open to criticism. There were those who thought he should have made a fight of it, feeling that the *Graf Spee* was not so badly damaged as to have prevented her making a breakout.

With hindsight, he might just have pulled it off, but Langsdorff had to consider what could have been waiting for him outside the sanctuary of Montevideo. The reports about reinforcements might have been enough to confirm any doubts in Langsdorff's mind. It might, too, have been that he considered it a fruitless exercise to risk the loss of so many young lives in a final gesture of defiance that, in his reasoning, could have but little chance of success. Whatever the reason, Langsdorff did not lack courage in his final act—shooting himself. He had not gone down with his ship, as some thought he should have done—but was not his act of self-destruction a braver, more cold-blooded thing?

The end for Langsdorff came while he and his remaining crew were accommodated in Buenos Aires. Late in the evening of 19th December, Langsdorff wrote a letter to the German Ambassador in Buenos Aires. It said, in part:

"After a long struggle, I reached the grave decision to scuttle the pocket battleship *Graf Spee* in order to prevent her from falling into the hands of the enemy. I am convinced that no other course was open to me, once I had taken my ship into the trap of Montevideo."

He concluded: "I can now only prove by my death that the fighting services of the Third Reich are ready to die for the honour of the flag. I alone bear responsibility for scuttling the pocket battleship *Admiral Graf Spee*. I am happy to pay with my life for any possible reflection on the honour of the flag. I shall face my fate with firm faith in the cause and the future of the nation and my Fuehrer."

The following morning he was found shot dead by his own hand. His body was wrapped in an old Imperial German Navy ensign. He was buried in the German cemetery in Buenos Aires.

So ended the life of a German Naval officer who was in some ways a man out of his time. He had, perhaps, a too chivalrous streak in him.

He had taken nine ships as prizes and considered the safety of their crews when that very consideration was likely to put his own ship in jeopardy. His action in putting ashore the *Clement*'s crew had alerted the British Admiralty to the fact that a German raider was at large in the South Atlantic.

The tactics he adopted would have no place in the savage conflicts that were to be waged in the North Atlantic and on the Russian convoy run. Now Langsdorff had made his own peace. It takes courage of a special kind for a man to shoot himself in cold blood for what he considers a matter of honour.

On the British side, the affair was a matter for rejoicing. Commodore Harwood received a signal during the wait outside Montevideo announcing his promotion to the rank of rear-admiral. It was a proud moment for him and for his crews.

With the *Graf Spee* out of the way, Winston Churchill, in his capacity as First Lord of the Admiralty, wanted to get the hunting groups—their task now finished—home as quickly as possible. He was particularly concerned about the *Exeter*. The cruiser, which had suffered heavy casualties in the battle, more than fifty officers and men being killed and a score wounded, was in the Falkland Islands. Churchill bitterly opposed the idea that she should remain there without being repaired until the end of the war. The *Exeter* came home and died gallantly against the Japanese in the Battle of the Java Sea on 1st March 1942.

Apart from the practical aspect of freeing the South Atlantic of a raider that had tied up units of the Royal Navy that could ill be spared, the Battle of the River Plate gave a tremendous boost to the British people. Their standing was high in the world. The British had shown that they could hand out punishment as well as take it. Even Langsdorff had been quoted as saying while the world waited for the final act: "The cruisers made a gallant fight. When people fight like that, personal enmity is lost."

There was one jarring note in the affair. The American Republics made a formal protest to Britain, France and Germany about the action. They claimed that it was a violation of the American Security Zone. Churchill replied to President Roosevelt and said the British action had been to the advantage of the republics in that the South Atlantic was now free of harassment by a commerce raider.

The releasing of the British Merchant Navy officers at Montevideo had also been the means of disclosing the information about the crews of the merchant ships now listed as overdue. They were being held in the *Altmark*, which had been supplying the *Graf Spee* with fuel and stores, the released prisoners reported as they stepped ashore in Montevideo. She was, they said, lurking in the South Atlantic and had had several meetings with the pocket battleship.

Churchill suggested to the First Sea Lord, Admiral Sir Dudley Pound, that those forces returning home should "scrub and search" the South Atlantic for the elusive *Altmark*. So began another hunt.

5

Ghost of the South Atlantic

The ship that Churchill had said the returning naval forces should "scrub and search" the South Atlantic for was now lurking in the ocean wastes. Dau now knew, as did his crew, that the *Graf Spee* had met her end at Montevideo. They had learned this from the radio broadcasts that had been streaming out to the world as commentators gave a running account of the events at Montevideo. The prisoners did not know anything officially, but guessed from the demeanour of Dau, his officers and the *Spee* guards that something was wrong.

Rumour was rife, and the men taking their turn at bringing food to the flats seized on any sign that could give them a clue as to what was happening.

Melville-Evans had started a diary in the blank pages of a bankbook issued by the Cardiff branch of the National Provincial Bank Limited in the name of William Melville-Evans, Esq., and giving his address in Penarth, Glamorgan. The clerk who made out deposit account No. 8524 could never have suspected that the simple book would be transformed into a prisoner's "log" of the voyage of the *Altmark*.

His entry for Saturday, 16th December, read:

> Today it is two weeks since the *Doric Star* was sunk and things are just about the same. We hear lots of rumours of what they intend to do with us, and what the *Graf Spee* is doing, but nothing definite. We have heard that the *Graf Spee* is sunk.
>
> This week I shifted from the carpeting and slung a hammock in the middle of a lot of empty beer barrels and big shell carriers. The hammock is made from sacking, but it is very comfortable. Today they painted out the name *Sogne* and changed the name to *Haugesund*.

This was another Norwegian name under which the *Altmark* had chosen to sail as she entered on the new phase of the deadly game of hide and seek. She was well and truly alone, and Dau knew it. "We shall have to do our best," he said to Paulsen. "Kapitaen Langsdorff put up a glorious fight, but in the end decided that it was more prudent to scuttle than to fight against overwhelming British forces. He saved many lives by his action, but for himself chose to die for the honour of the flag. Now we shall have the British Navy on to us. We must do everything we can to take the *Altmark* back to Germany. It is our duty," he declared, dismissing Paulsen with a wave of his hand.

The chief officer left, thinking to himself that they would be lucky to escape detection. The other officers also had their own thoughts on the subject.

All the prisoners had now settled into a routine. Those who had been captured first were feeling the captivity more than those who had been taken aboard the *Altmark* early in December. Melville-Evans and Wally Wells were among the fortunate ones who had been captured late on.

Strangely enough, Melville-Evans did not find life boring. He found himself too busy as there always seemed to be something to do just to keep things shipshape. There was the daily wash, the washing of clothes, entering up the diary and seeing that his hammock and personal belongings were kept in order.

One problem for the smokers among the captives was that of cigarettes and tobacco. They had brought some with them from their respective ships. Though the fifth deck was what might be termed a smoke room, where smoking was allowed, matches being supplied at the rate of one box every second day, it was otherwise prohibited to smoke. The penalty was solitary confinement with a diet of bread and water. The shortage of cigarettes became so acute as the days passed that some men were driven to bartering belongings for a few cigarettes.

One man in the officer's flat was so desperate for a smoke that he plucked pieces of jute from the floor and stuffed them into his pipe. He lit up and at once the flat was filled with acrid fumes that brought curses from those around him. "For God's sake put that damn thing out," they shouted out.

It was to no avail. The man went on smoking, almost choking on his pipe as he smoked. "I've got to have a smoke, lads, and even jute tastes better than nothing at all," he apologized as he puffed himself red in the face. "Get caught, and you'll end up in the cooler," one man shouted across the flat as he shielded his nose from the stench of the jute that smouldered in the offending smoker's pipe.

One man who had been caught smoking was the chief steward of the

Tairoa, J. C. Smith, who spent three days in "solitary" and had to exist on bread and water.

At least there was some consolation in solitary confinement—it meant that a man could be alone for a time instead of being cooped up with his fellow prisoners in the flats.

Some who put a brave face on things during the day as they laughed and joked with their companions, or grumbled at the conditions, fought their own private battle as they dozed or tried to sleep on the carpeting after lights out. Loneliness came upon them, and they wondered about their families at home. They were accustomed to being away from home for long periods, but this was something different. There were no letters or parcels for them as in a normal prison camp, nor did they even know if their families knew that they were alive. There were men, too, who wondered about their wives only to curse themselves for being so disloyal. The isolation and uncertainty preyed on men's nerves. Action, any action, was preferable to being imprisoned in a tanker that in a way was now a prisoner herself.

One fortunate aspect of the situation was that the *Huntsman*'s crew had been allowed to bring all their belongings to the *Altmark*. They had with them books, nautical tables and playing cards. The result was that the prisoners were able to get card schools going, while the books were passed from hand to hand to become steadily the worse for wear. There were games, too, that the captives improvised for themselves.

Dr Tyrolt made his daily inspections and professed himself surprised at how well the prisoners were despite the conditions. There were the usual minor complaints, aches and pains and stomach upsets, but nothing to cause any concern. Tyrolt was thankful for he knew that he would be in difficulties if he got a really serious case on his hands.

The Lascars were also bearing up well in the alien conditions. They prepared their own food and followed their own customs. The German cook, Schwill, and the baker, Treibel, could not appreciate the diet of the Indians. "Give me good old German sausage any time," said Schwill. "I couldn't stomach that rice stuff," he remarked to Treibel.

But food was not so plentiful that the Germans and captives could pick and choose. Third Officer Schmidt cursed yet another helping of macaroni and vowed that he would never let his wife, Lilly, serve him with it if he ever reached home again. He often thought of Lilly, whom he had married on 27th May 1939. "Is it only so long ago?" he reflected as he thought that in a few days it would be Christmas. It would be a quiet Christmas for Lilly. For him it would be just another day at sea; another day on watch, wondering, waiting. The war went on, even if they seemed remote from it all.

Schmidt's wife, however, was aware that her husband was safe. After the sinking of the *Graf Spee* the German Admiralty had informed relatives of the crew that all in the *Altmark* were well. His wife, he learned later, thought the *Altmark* had been interned. The problem was that while the *Altmark* could receive messages from the S.K.L.—Seekriegsleitung—in Berlin, the tanker dare not reply for fear of disclosing her position. The messages from S.K.L. were decoded and acted upon if necessary. For the rest, the *Altmark*, which had been close to the Equator when the *Graf Spee* was cornered, went her own way.

Thoughts of Christmas were also on the minds of the prisoners. Melville-Evans took a laconic view of things, writing in his diary for Saturday, 23rd December:

> Well, here is the third week [since his capture] and it is the last shopping day before Christmas. And to mark the occasion, they have cut down our ration of black bread, of which we get a day's allowance every night. But for the two meals the next day it is soggy and sour. We would have been home easily had we not met Jerry. We stopped on Thursday and have been drifting ever since.

There was a bright note on Christmas Eve that meant a lot to the captives. It was announced that it had been made known in England that the crews of the ships sunk by the *Graf Spee* were saved. The notice Dau had had posted in the flat read:

> About all ships sunk by the *Admiral Graf Spee* until the end of November, including the *Doric Star* and *Tairoa*, it has been made known in England that the crews were saved.
>
> December 24th, 1939

"That's a grand Christmas present anyway," said Archibald Willis, the *Doric Star*'s second mate, as someone started to sing carols. Soon the whole flat was singing away. It was good to know that relatives at home knew that they were safe, even if they did not know where they were. It relieved the prisoners of the nagging anxiety that their families may have come to the conclusion that they were dead. The fact that they now knew they were safe put new heart into the prisoners as they sang one carol after another. From the sound, it could have been in an English country church instead of in a tanker wallowing in the South Atlantic swell.

Conditions were worsening. Dau had called his officers together after they had learned of the end of the *Graf Spee*. "Gentlemen," he told them, "we are now alone. We must now consider what is the safest course for us to take if the *Altmark* is not to be taken by the British. It is too dangerous to make a break for Germany now while the British forces are still sweeping the South Atlantic after the scuttling of the *Graf Spee*."

"Herr Kapitaen," said Paulsen, "it would perhaps be best if we could hide for a few weeks until the British move away or think we have already slipped through the net." There was a general murmur of assent.

The chief engineer, Schleusner, spoke up. "Herr Kapitaen, it is impossible to make the return voyage without overhauling the engines. They are badly in need of repair. We cannot sail home without attending to the engines."

Dau had to concede that. He knew, like the captains of all ships of whatever nationality, that when an engineer gave his views about anything relating to engines, those views had to be taken into account. Schleusner nursed the engines like a baby, and now he wanted time to do repairs. They had been at sea since leaving Germany in August, apart from their short stay at Port Arthur, and the position was becoming serious.

Other officers spoke up, and it was agreed that the best course would be to run at full speed for the South to hide in the icy and foggy waters of the Antarctic where repairs could be carried out.

"To your duties, then," said Dau as he dismissed his officers. He realized this was the only sensible course open to them if they were to have any chance of ever reaching Germany. The British had caught the *Graf Spee*, but he would try his best to see that the *Altmark* returned home safely.

The cold was now being felt in the prisoners' flats. Christmas Day found Melville-Evans writing this in his diary:

Damn nearly freezing. As usual we get up at 6 a.m. and bathe in a bowl of water on deck. Breakfast of bread, butter and tea is helped by an officer from the *Tairoa* producing a few tins of bully beef that he had stowed away.

For dinner we were given a treat. First some thin soup, then rabbit, macaroni and beans. Afterwards some tinned goosegogs. Everyone was well satisfied after the usual stuff dished up. For tea, we were back to normal with black bread and sausage. And so our Christmas Day was over. The prisoner officer gave us our present last night when he told us that people in England had been informed that we are all safe.

The Germans did the best they could to celebrate Christmas. The remaining supplies of chocolates and cigarettes were distributed among them. The baker and cook tried to liven up the menu. There was little they could do, however, with the limited supplies they had. They also did not know how long they would have to last.

In the prisoners' flats, Christmas or not, the talk was often of escape. There were wild schemes for overpowering the guards and crew and taking over the ship. The wiser heads said that such a course would be doomed to failure from the start. Many prisoners would certainly be killed before they could seize the weapons.

"There must be something we can do," one of the prisoners remarked as the talk of escape went on and on.

It was then that the idea of a message was born. What if they could get a message over the side? It might be picked up by some ship and the *Altmark*'s position passed on to the Admiralty. It was a slim chance, but it was worth taking. After all, had not bottle messages cast into the sea drifted for months and then been washed up intact on some shore? Many items about such messages had appeared in the newspapers at various times.

It was one thing to toss a bottle containing a message into the sea in the ordinary way, but it was another to do it from a prison ship. The Germans were strict about anything being thrown overboard. There was always the fear that it would give away their presence. This had been a problem when the *Altmark* had been supplying the *Graf Spee* during their meetings. Strict precautions had always been taken to see that nothing was left floating—a box or timber—to act as a pointer to their having met.

How, then, were they to get it over the side without the Germans seeing it? Anyone throwing the message overboard would certainly be seen. The question was debated and several ideas were put forward before someone pointed out the one method that stood a good chance of success—the latrine drums. These were emptied each day by the captives themselves. Hidden in the drum, the message would go overboard with the contents.

Now that the method was settled, there came the problem of preparing the message and placing it in a container that would float for a considerable time. It must be able to withstand the sea.

On Christmas Day, Wally Wells and others set to work to prepare the message. A container was fashioned from an empty cocoa tin. Inside was placed a typewritten S.O.S. message, stating its origin and giving the approximate position of the *Altmark*. This was then placed inside the latrine and the two men on fetch-and-carry duty from the flats emptied the latrine drum over the side. The container had been waterproofed by bandages and bore a flag on a five-inch stick.

The men who had emptied the drum hurried back across the deck, but as they prepared to descend there was a shout from the lookout on the port wing. He had spotted the box bobbing in the sea, its flag flying bravely. Immediately, the bridge signalled stop engines. The *Altmark* hove to, a boat was lowered, the offending box retrieved with a boat hook and brought on board.

Dau, pacing the bridge while this was in progress, smiled as the box was broken open. In addition to giving the approximate position of the *Altmark*, the message said there were on board 300 British crew members and that the ship was fitted with guns.

"Paulsen, the prisoners must be taught a lesson," said Dau, whose smile had now gone. "Get the prisoners to the forecastle." The prisoners stumbled out of the flats wondering what was going on, for most of them were not aware of the attempt to get a message over the side.

They were soon left in no doubt. Dau abused them and said they must be taught a lesson. Rations would be cut, there would be no tea, only water, and exercise on deck would be cancelled for two days. Inwardly, however, Dau was impressed by the attempt. It was the sort of thing he liked to think he would have done himself in similar circumstances. He fully realized that had the tin not been seen the *Altmark* could easily have been betrayed. He made a mental note to commend the port wing lookout for his alertness. Such vigilance was necessary for their survival. It was agreed by those prisoners concerned that they would not tell Otto Schmidt who were the culprits, but to take the blame as a whole. The officers from the bridge who had observed the episode went through the flats trying to recognize the men who had emptied the latrines, but failed to do so.

Lieutenant Schmidt reminded them that night that during the First World War the German raider *Wolf* was almost captured through a similar message. Without rancour, he told them: "You will understand that we cannot take undue risks. You yourselves would take the same precautions in our position."

The incident of the message gave Melville-Evans an entry for his diary. On Boxing Day, 26th December, he wrote: "Because of the box thrown over the side, we have to stay below decks without exercise."

On Tuesday, 27th December, he was writing:

> Well, we wake up today and are told that we are to be kept confined to our flat for three days, not even being allowed to wash. So we undoubtedly spent Boxing Day indoors. Now later in the day we are told our exercise period will (in three days' time) be restricted to 50 minutes every other day. So that makes an average of 25 minutes a day against an hour and a quarter. Also, the chief steward of the *Tairoa* was caught smoking by a guard and received three days' solitary confinement with a bread and water diet.

Being forbidden to wash for a time was not too much of a hardship in those latitudes. The washing arrangements were only crude at the best of times. The German Navy soap was in short supply and of poor quality. It needed a great deal of effort to work up a lather, particularly as the water used was partly salt.

One of the decks had been cleaned out and was called the "hospital", which was an apology for the name, considering the spartan conditions there. One crew member from the *Tairoa* who was injured in the foot when the ship was fired on by the *Graf Spee* was kept permanently in the hospital as it was difficult for him to use the ladders to the other decks. Apart from this, the only patients were a steward, who was a suspected case of appendicitis, but which turned out to be a false alarm, and from time to time a Lascar whose food had upset him.

The Lascars, of whom there were about seventy, bore the conditions with remarkable fortitude, although there was for them the added difficulty that they did not understand the situation in the way the British did. They were fortunate in that they had brought their own supplies of food from the *Huntsman* before she was sunk. Had they not been able to do this, they would have been in difficulties, their religion calling for special food.

After the scuttling of the *Graf Spee*, the *Altmark*, in her guise as the *Haugesund*, had steamed south at about 15 knots and had continued on this course until she had reached 58 or 59 degrees south latitude and then remained there just cruising about in mountainous seas and freezing blizzards.

Conditions in the flats were atrocious. The prisoners were not allowed on deck because of the weather. The heat from their bodies helped to cause condensation from the deckheads, so that the captives had to suffer a constant drip-drip of moisture on to their bodies. Their blankets—most of them had only one each—were also sodden, which made things even more uncomfortable. In spite of this, they managed to keep up their spirits.

Just how high their spirits were was demonstrated to the Germans when, one night, with midnight just an hour away, one of the doors giving access to the prisoners' decks creaked open and there was a rush of feet as a group of prisoners tried to overcome the crewman acting as watchman. But they were not quick enough and the Germans underneath the forecastle deck drove them back with high-pressure water-hoses.

Now the alarm was well and truly raised and the prisoners had no option but to return to their flats, soaked through and cursing their luck. Had they succeeded in breaking out, there would still have been the question of gaining control of the ship from armed men, who would no doubt have inflicted a heavy toll among the British as they scattered around the deck.

Dau was furious and demanded to know how the prisoners had managed to break out of a deck that was supposedly secure, and ordered an investigation. It was discovered that one of the Indians had been given a gold coin by one of the British officers and used this to wedge the door open a fraction. Watch was kept through the crack provided by the wedged coin, and as the ship settled down for the night the prisoners took their chance to try to break out. Just who exactly was responsible for the affair of the coin, Dau was unable to discover, but the incident proved that the Indians were more loyal to the British than he had suspected.

"We must keep a close watch on them," he told Third Officer Schmidt. "They seem to be more loyal to their officers than I thought."

It was a warning to Dau that however things might seem on the surface, there was an undercurrent of unrest among the prisoners that could break out into a mass escape attempt if matters were not kept under control. Another attempt at getting a message away had been thwarted, though even a successful "launch" would have given the message little hope of being spotted, or even surviving in the rough seas that were running.

The constant cold as 1939 drew to a close was making things even more uncomfortable in the flats. It was a struggle to keep warm. Melville-Evans and his fellow officers cut up several of the Indian carpets in the flat and used them as eiderdowns.

The *Doric Star*'s third mate noted in his diary for Saturday, 30th December:

> Hi, ho!, here is the fourth week as Jerry's prisoners. Some of the fellows here [those taken prisoner earlier] have nearly three months in. We have no cigarettes and we are not allowed to smoke in the flats. Haven't smoked since we came aboard. The old throat is better for it, but still pretty crook.

On New Year's Eve, the Britishers did their best to celebrate. As Melville-Evans wrote:

> We saw the New Year in at midnight with a good show of songs, and made a New Year resolution to be bad prisoners. Still, there is very little we can do, being shut up practically all the time. I should think the crew of this ship are pretty fed up as they have been struck out in the South Atlantic for five months.

It was important that they kept active so far as the limitations of the flats allowed. It did not do just to sit and brood. Minds and bodies had to be exercised as best they could.

The prisoners got many games going. The men from the *Huntsman* had with them a few packs of cards, supplemented by others provided by the *Graf Spee* guards. There was also a set of chess pieces for the chess fans. Half a dozen darts were used constantly by those who liked a game of darts. With the aid of pencils, penknives and pieces of wood, they soon had a chess board and darts board. One of the decks also had a draughts board made from a piece of steel plate about two feet square, and for "pieces" used three-quarter inch nuts they found in their deck. The captives found it most amusing to see two of their number carrying the heavy "board" to one corner of their deck for a quiet game of draughts, but it served its purpose. Other draughts games were made from wood, the pieces being cut from a broom handle and the board marked with a pencil.

Ludo games and race games were fashioned from pieces of cardboard, the dice being a hexagonal piece of cardboard, which was spun on a matchstick through its centre.

For greater comfort in the flats, some men even made shoes from canvas and rope provided by Lieutenant Schmidt, while others set patiently to work to make Dutch "sabots".

When the weather was too bad for them to have exercises on deck, they enjoyed games such as leap-frog and put themselves through their paces with indoor exercises. The decks, as ammunition stores, were all fitted with overhead sprinkler pipes in case of fire and also with cooling pipes, and these made "gym" bars on which to swing.

The exercises played a big part in keeping the men fit. The difficulty was that those who were not exercising had to give up their beds for those who were.

Despite the exercises to keep them fit, there was still some sickness among the prisoners, but fortunately nothing serious. Dr Tyrolt, however, continued to be worried over the lack of medical supplies and the poor sanitary conditions. He earned the thanks of the captives for the manner in which he did all he could to help them. Those whose stomachs would not take the usual food he put on special soft food diets, mostly porridge. He also did what he could to have the lavatories screened off from the living quarters.

Although the weather was cold, the order forbidding washing for several days after the discovery of the S.O.S. message had not helped in matters of hygiene. Before the Christmas Day message "plot", the men had all washed on deck each morning. They had been able to heat up their water at a small steam hose near the forward "pump house", but the discovery of the message had ended washing over the Christmas period.

"I feel lousy," said one man as he felt the stubble on his chin. But it was agreed that Dau had done the right thing from his point of view in stopping them from washing on deck. They knew they would take any chance they could to get a message away, and being allowed on deck to wash was just the opportunity to slip something over the side.

Melville-Evans was busy with his diary again. On Saturday, 6th January, he was writing:

> The first week has passed without any stirring events. There has even been a lack of rumours, not that anyone takes much notice of them. But they do make something to yarn about. The one about the battleship being sunk seems to be correct unless she has gone back to Jerryland. Anyway,

she has not been back to this ship for exactly one month, and here we have been cruising round in the desolation of the Southern Ocean ever since.

Rumours had been what the men had lived on ever since coming aboard. They got what information they could from talking with Schmidt and Tyrolt and from watching for signs of extra activity on board. Visits to the galley also led to their share of rumours. The cook and the *Altmark* purser, Brautigam, were both fat, cheerful men. They would talk and laugh with the prisoners when the "duty men" were collecting the rations.

By one of those quirks of fate, the *Altmark* purser and the chief steward of the *Tairoa*, Smith, knew each other. The purser had served with the North German Lloyd Line as chief steward in one of their Western Ocean passenger ships long before the outbreak of war. The fact that they were now enemies did not in any way lessen the friendship. They enjoyed chats about old times whenever the opportunity arose. Brautigam had joined the *Altmark* in December 1938.

The day of 13th January, dawned with no change in the routine. It marked the beginning of the sixth week of captivity for the crew of the *Doric Star*. Archibald Willis, the *Doric Star*'s second mate, whose home was in Ilford, Essex, passed the time by doing saucy drawings that amused the others in his flat. His drawings were also skilful and drew admiration from his fellow captives. It was obvious that his talent was such as to enable him to make a career outside the Merchant Navy.

His talents at drawing created a welcome diversion. For it was, said Melville-Evans in his diary,

one of the most uneventful weeks sence we were taken prisoner. We are certainly well South in the cold weather and all the iron work is sweating, causing everything to be very damp. Very heavy seas are running continuously sending spray over all.

The "Cherub" [Lieutenant Schmidt] issued us with our last cake of soap. When this is gone, I don't know what we shall have to do.

A week later he was writing:

Well, as a lazy life, this takes some beating. Stay in bed all day, have meals brought to you. Even if you get up, there is nothing to do except talk and maybe a game of cards, although it is very seldom I play.

Passing the time may have been the hardest task for the prisoners, but for Dau there was the problem of preparing for the "march to Germany". The time was near for the *Altmark*'s breakout.

6

Attack Cape Town

Heavy seas were running and it was bitterly cold as Chief Officer Paulsen and Third Officer Schmidt walked the bridge of the *Altmark*, still "sailing to nowhere" in the South Atlantic. Below decks, the prisoners were doing their best to keep warm and dry as the iron-work streamed with condensation. Spray whipped across the deck and Paulsen and Schmidt shivered in the bleakness of it all.

It was now well into January 1940. Dau had been growing impatient. He had wanted to be away from this desolate spot. Yet he knew they could not just sail straight away without preparations. The first engineer, Schleusner, had made it clear that the engines needed attention.

"We have sailed many miles, Herr Kapitaen," the first engineer had told Dau. "I cannot guarantee the speed when you want it unless I am given time to overhaul the engines. We shall need them to be in good condition if we are to outwit the Tommies," he said, using the word *Tommies* to describe the British.

Accordingly, Schleusner and his men set to work, but not without attracting the attention of the prisoners with all the banging and clanging that was going on. Engine parts were brought up on deck where necessary for cleaning and overhauling. The men from the flats carrying out galley duties brought back reports of Germans struggling with the heavy metal parts in atrocious conditions.

"What the devil's going on?" said Chief Steward Smith, of the *Tairoa*, now back in the flats again after his solitary confinement for smoking. He was more used to cutlery than pistons and the pieces of machinery were all a mystery to him.

Archibald Willis, another mystified by the world of machinery, was not much interested in the activity, but it gave him and the others something to talk about.

"I bet the blighter's getting ready for a run for Germany," said Melville-Evans, whose view was backed up by the engineers among the officers. They took a professional interest in the matter. They realized that the *Altmark* had been at sea so long she was in no condition to face the North Atlantic weather in the state her engines must be in after the months at sea.

The prisoners were also tired of being cooped up below decks. It was now several weeks since they had been out in the daylight, and all of them were beginning to show signs of it in their faces, which were paler than usual. The Indian crew of the *Huntsman* were also suffering in that they were short of curry and rice.

The only news the prisoners could glean came from chance remarks dropped by the guards and by what those doing mess duty could pick up on their trips to the galley. For the rest, the prisoners had to while away the hours as best they could. The artificial light was also proving something of a strain on their eyes, but generally their health remained good.

Melville-Evans paid tribute to Dr Tyrolt in a diary entry: "The doctor is a good sort and would be useful if he had any medicine."

He also noted: "The Germans certainly dislike Winston Churchill." They cursed him, and the British only made them more angry by baiting them with such remarks as "Winnie will get us out of this. You'll see. He'll have the Navy down on you, and then it will be you lot who will be the prisoners."

Lieutenant Schmidt was often at the receiving end of this, but "Babyface", or the "Cherub", as he was also known, usually managed to keep calm. It was also at such times that he was questioned as to what would happen to the prisoners if the *Altmark* were attacked by the Royal Navy or aircraft. Would they be left to die like rats in a trap? he was asked.

Babyface was always at pains to assure them that the safety of the prisoners was of prime consideration. Every effort would be made to ensure their safety if the *Altmark* ran into danger.

The *Altmark* carried only six lifeboats and some liferafts. There were also ladders, empty fuel drums and other objects that could be used to keep men afloat in an emergency. An enemy warship would also be sent a message not to shoot as prisoners were in the holds and to send boats to pick them up. They would not be able to board the ship as preparations had been made to burn and sink the *Altmark* within five minutes. Any attempt at boarding would bring about the immediate destruction of the ship. It sounded all right, but as someone pointed out: "What if it's a submarine that spots us and isn't fooled by any false name. A couple of torpedoes and we'll go up like a Brock's Benefit."

Not only were the engines overhauled, but other work was done to make the tanker ready for the long voyage that lay ahead. Marine growth had also fouled the hull and a list had to be given to the *Altmark*, first at one side and then at the other, in order that the growth could be removed. It was hard and hazardous work in the conditions. The rudder and both propellers were also cleaned. Screens were fitted on to the funnel to prevent engine sparks betraying the ship in darkness. The crew also got to work with paint from the large stores the *Altmark* carried and gave the ship a new guise. She became the *Chiriqui*.

The prisoners had been exchanging gossip and rumours on what was happening. They had heard the engines start up and the propellers begin to turn. The *Altmark* had then undergone "trials" to test the engines and to see how seaworthy was the ship. Even the most pessimistic of the prisoners was now forced to agree that something was happening after the several weeks spent in that desolate region.

The long-awaited dash for Germany began on 24th January, when a murmur ran through the flats as the *Altmark*'s engines began a purposeful throb. "We're off," Melville-Evans exclaimed. "Another trial, likely," said Wally Wells. After so long, it seemed hard to believe that this might be the real thing.

There was now no doubt about it. The steady rhythm continued, and it was estimated the *Altmark* was doing some 15 knots. The rumour about the breakout for Germany was now apparently correct. (The *Altmark* was actually doing 19 knots, but without maximum revolutions.)

With the *Altmark* moving again, the topic of what the prisoners could do to outwit the Germans was once more given emphasis, though it had never been far from their minds. They just had to do something, it was felt. They had long realized that it would be courting suicide to try to overcome the guards, who would not hesitate to shoot. Lieutenant Schmidt was a decent sort, but he was a loyal German and would not shirk his duty.

The officers decided that, while they could not hope to beat the Germans in an open clash, there was a way they could put one over them. Melville-Evans still had the magnetic variation chart of the Atlantic he had taken with him from the *Doric Star* to the *Graf Spee* and then to the *Altmark*. There had been no serious attempt to check their belongings—what few they possessed were hardly worth checking—and so he had kept the chart. The sextants carried by the navigating officers had been confiscated when they had taken them aboard the *Graf Spee*, but the Germans had acted with strict correctness and issued receipts for the equipment. The charts carried by the other officers had also been taken away. That kept by the *Doric Star*'s third officer was the only one the prisoners had.

Now began the "shadowing" of the *Altmark*'s voyage. "We'll track the Germans," said Melville-Evans as he spread out the chart in the confines of the flat. A system was then organized by which they could observe the German navigators through the after trunkway "peephole" under the bridge as they took sights at noon. Three of the British officers used a card with a pin, the card being marked out like a protractor. One officer held the card and sighted it, one kept it horizontal and the third read off. Melville-Evans kept the chart. A copy of Brown's nautical almanac brought aboard by one of the navigating officers was used to find the longitude.

Dau was unaware of all this activity close at hand as he watched his officers going about their duties and taking sights. He believed he had thwarted the prisoners in their efforts to get messages overboard, but he never realized that the captives were dogging what could be termed the *Altmark*'s very "footsteps". The routine of charting the tanker's position continued daily and gave a sense of purpose to the men in the officers' flat. They also thought that if ever the Royal Navy rescued them, the chart could be of some use to the Admiralty. (This assumption was to prove correct.)

There was a new feeling in the flats now that the *Altmark* had started her breakout. Endless discussions took place on the chances of the tanker being intercepted by the Royal Navy. It was believed that there was a strong patrol covering the area between Dakar, West Africa, and Pernambuco, Brazil.

"For all the Navy knows, the *Altmark* could be back in Germany," Wally Wells said as the officers debated the possibility of rescue. "They could long since have given up the search. They may even think we have been sunk."

Others disagreed, refusing to give up hope that every effort was being made to locate them. The Navy must also know that the *Altmark* was using a disguise after the release of prisoners from the *Graf Spee* at Montevideo.

The Navy would certainly have found them if the *Altmark*'s officers had agreed with the plan put to them by Dau. Before the *Altmark* began her homeward run, he called a conference.

"Gentlemen," he said, "now that we are to leave this area, it seems to me that we should try to strike a blow for the Fatherland. Our engines are now repaired and we have guns and ammunition and we are able to make good speed. Our glorious *Graf Spee* struck a blow against the Tommies, both in capturing merchant ships and in damaging their warships. Now, alas, she is with us no longer, but perhaps we can do something to prove that we are of more value than a mere supply ship."

He paused and gazed at his officers, a thin smile on his lips as he took in their bewildered expressions. Third Officer Schmidt wondered if he was going to come up with a scheme as mad as that concerning the capture of a submarine. Chief Officer Paulsen had already had enough of Dau's moods since the *Graf Spee* had been scuttled, while Second Officers de Harde, Schroder, Rummler and Garte were in no mood for a madcap adventure that was likely to end in death for some of them. First Engineer Schleusner wondered what new demands were to be put on his beloved engines.

A moment had passed since Dau had spoken, but it seemed an age to the assembled officers. Their thoughts were cut short as Dau announced: "I propose that we make an attack on Cape Town. We could shoot at installations on shore and also shoot at ships there. We could strike a blow for Germany and show them that not only is the *Altmark* still sailing freely, but also that she is capable of striking a blow for the Fuehrer."

Immediately, a babble of voices broke out, only to be silenced as Dau held up his hand. "It is a proposal and I would like your views on it," he said before lapsing into silence.

The officers looked at each other, and then Paulsen spoke. "Herr Kapitaen," he began, "I respect your wishes to serve our country still further, but, with respect, I would suggest this would be a dangerous thing to do. We have also our prisoners to consider."

Then de Harde spoke: "I, too, must agree with Herr Paulsen. I would also point out that we have no charts of Cape Town, and that we have no range-finder."

Third Officer Schmidt added his weight to the argument, secretly thinking that Dau was seeking glory for himself and also a decoration. He wanted to be a hero instead of the captain of an obscure tanker, even if she was now being hunted by the British Navy.

Paulsen also pointed out that even if they did manage to inflict some damage, which he felt would not be very great, they would bring down on them the might of the British Navy. Cruisers and destroyers would seek them out, and in no time at all the *Altmark* would be a blazing wreck and sink within minutes. Many of the crew and prisoners would no doubt be killed in the attack or drowned as the *Altmark* sank. The world generally would be amazed at the foolhardy action of a prison ship going into battle.

"We shall achieve nothing but death for many of us," said Gustav Garte. His view met with nods of approval. Others also expressed their opinions, all pointing out the obvious dangers that such a venture must incur.

Dau leaned back in his chair, the smile now gone. He fingered his beard for a moment then stood up. "I will bow to your views, gentlemen. There are dangers, I must admit, but I had hoped we could have distinguished ourselves instead of slinking away.

"That is settled then. We do not attack Cape Town, but make all speed for Germany. At least if we can get the *Altmark* home, we shall live to fight another day, as the saying is. Whether we get the *Altmark* home will depend on us all. We must keep a sharp lookout and take all avoiding action if we see any other ships. And I must insist that the prisoners are kept under the strictest supervision. We do not want any more messages to get overboard. We may not be so lucky next time at spotting any attempt.

"I want our comrade from the *Graf Spee*, Lieutenant Schmidt, to see that his guards keep the closest watch on the prisoners. We do not know what they plot while they are in the flats. As we get nearer home, we can expect more attempts to give away the *Altmark*'s position.

"I shall not rest until we have the *Altmark* safely back at Kiel and the prisoners are transferred to a prisoner-of-war camp. We have treated them as well as possible in the conditions. We do not have the facilities that the *Graf Spee* had. We can only do the best we can. We must be firm and stand no nonsense from them. The safety of the ship depends on our firmness. We must be alert for any attempted breakout. At least now that we are not to attack Cape Town, we can give our full attention to the prisoners and to getting back to Germany." He dismissed them.

Rain lashed down as de Harde strode the bridge and pondered on Dau's plan to attack Cape Town before he had given way to the views of his officers. It was just another incident on a cruise that seemed doomed to go wrong. There had been the trouble with the authorities in Port Arthur before sailing to meet the *Graf Spee*, and in the end they had been saddled with all the prisoners. The month of hiding in the South Atlantic had not helped matters. Both men and officers, he reflected, were getting near the end of their tether. It was to be hoped that they would manage to avoid the Tommies on their run for Germany. It would be good to be home again, but what they would find there after the months of war he did not know.

Paulsen, Garte, Walter Schmidt and the other officers were all busy with their own thoughts. It would have been a disaster to have attacked Cape Town, they thought. "Just think, a tanker trying to escape from a destroyer or a cruiser, even if we did inflict some damage before trying to escape," thought Schmidt. They would be lucky enough as it was to get through the British patrols unseen without indulging in schemes such as that proposed by Dau.

But there was work to be done. Paulsen turned to Schmidt and told him: "See that a sharp lookout is kept." Lookouts were stationed on the bridge, decks, bridge wings and the compass deck. It was vital that the *Altmark* saw the smoke from a funnel or the tip of a mast before the other ship spotted them. They must also watch for waste and slops in the water—tell-tale signs of the passing of another vessel.

Twice the *Altmark* had to take swift avoiding action to increase the distance between them and another ship the alert lookouts had spotted. The narrows and the area between Freetown and Dakar and Recife, Brazil, were particularly dangerous, as Dau feared they would be spotted by aircraft he expected to be operating from Dakar.

The wireless operators, Thurz, Wendt and Luka, kept a round-the-clock watch. They turned into the frequencies of British and French merchant ships and also warships. They were also able to intercept messages from a Royal Navy wireless station in Great Britain. They listened for any mention of the *Altmark*, but learned little. They sailed on, maintaining radio silence and hoping that their alertness, coupled with a little luck, would see them through this dangerous area.

In the flats, the prisoners tried to pump Lieutenant Schmidt and Dr Tyrolt for information. Schmidt was only twenty-two and, it was felt, would have been more forthcoming had it not been for Dau. Schmidt had spent some years in England, and often chatted with the prisoners about their homes and countries. He was always willing to supply the prisoners with rope or canvas and other odds and ends with which they were able to make shoes for themselves. Once when he saw some men carving pieces of wood into model ships he said, "I will try to get you some materials." He was as good as his word, arriving in the officers' flat with paint, wood, tools and brushes.

They were little things, but they meant a lot to men who were locked up for long periods.

Dr Tyrolt also tried to make things as pleasant as he could for the prisoners, his efforts winning their friendship and admiration. He often visited the officers' flat half an hour before the morning inspection and would sit and chat with them until Schmidt had to drag him away for fear that he would tell them something he should not. He did the same with the men and the Lascars. His contact with the prisoners, he said, helped him with his desire to learn English.

Tyrolt, for all his intelligence and university training, had one flaw. German propaganda had got him so firmly in its grip that he was convinced that if he were taken prisoner by the British he would have his hands and feet cut off, and that this would be only one of the tortures he would suffer. Wally Wells and his comrades did all they could to convince him otherwise, but Tyrolt could not be persuaded.

Dau would also have been furious had he known just how much contact there was between the prisoners and Becker, the *Altmark*'s carpenter. He and the bosun were often at work near the flats and liked to talk with the Britishers. Their presence was doubly welcome for they slipped the captives tobacco and cigarettes, now in short supply and many of the men having none at all.

Wally Wells enjoyed talking with them and said jokingly to the bosun: "Soon we will be in Hamburg and then you'll be happy." He replied in broken English: "Hamburg all right. Yes! But Liverpool or Glasgow more better."

The reply was not altogether surprising. For Hamburg was notoriously anti-Nazi in that the population was largely seafaring and so had seen how people in other countries lived. The *Altmark*'s crew were no exception.

It was a different matter with the guards. They were very young and inexperienced, and only a few of them spoke English. They treated their charges with respect, but were not inclined to be friendly. They were, of course, under strict orders and any breach would have been severely dealt with.

As the ship rolled and pitched on her way to calmer waters, the prisoners kept up their spirits in all manner of ways. The time between the evening meal and roll-call at 7 p.m. was a period for enjoying themselves with community singing. They were accompanied by their own "band", which consisted of comb and tissue paper instruments and thumps on the hollow bulkheads to take the place of drums.

Often they would be in the middle of a rousing song when there would be a clatter of boots in the trunkway and Schmidt and the guards would appear for roll-call. "In line, in line," he would shout and the prisoners would get in four lines, two each side of the tables. It was then that "Babyface" would make announcements or give them news, or the German version of the news.

"Gentlemen," he would say, "I have to tell you that today 49 British ships have been sunk, 6 of them being destroyers. The winter in England has been the worst since 1935." The switch from the war news to the weather seemed incongruous, but he just gave snippets almost without pause.

The prisoners' reply to Schmidt's "news" was a polite "good evening" and then to break into song again with as much noise as possible. A popular choice was "Rule, Britannia", while at other times Schmidt and the guards were treated to a rousing rendering of "There'll always be an England".

Schmidt could tolerate the singing, even though it was defiant, but the young guards were not amused. They could not understand what the prisoners had to sing about. After all, they would soon be in prison in Germany.

Several of the prisoners had by now become acquainted with one of the "deep-tanks" in the *Altmark*. A deep-tank is a tank for storing oil. When one of these tanks became empty, it was cleaned out and used as a solitary confinement cell. Smoking on their own decks brought three days in the deep tank for anyone caught.

The punishment sounded worse than it was. For those sentenced to three days in the tank were allowed to take what bedding they had and also any books they possessed. It was not, therefore, too uncomfortable in the tank, which was spacious and electrically lit. It made it possible to get plenty of exercise and to enjoy reading while in "solitary". It was, in fact, more of a change than a punishment.

The attempts to get messages overboard went on in spite of the punishment that awaited the prisoners if they were caught in the act. The *Altmark*'s carpenter was an unwitting accessory in this, as the tins used for the messages were sealed with the paint and canvas that

The *Graf Spee* with one of her victims, the *Huntsman*

The end of the *Admiral Graf Spee* as she is scuttled at Montevideo (*BBC Hulton Picture Library*)

Captain Hans Langsdorff with members of his crew (*Imperial War Museum*)

Captain Heinrich Dau—master of the *Altmark*

The crew of the *Altmark* in March 1939: 1, Walter Schmidt; 2, Captain Dau; 3, Chief Engineer Schleusner

(*Above*) Third Officer William Melville-Evans in 1940

(*Above right*) Seventh Engineer W. F. Wells, of the *Tairoa*

(*Right*) Third Officer Walter Schmidt in 1940

(*Left*) The wheelhouse of the *Altmark*

(*Centre left*) The third officer's cabin in the *Altmark*

(*Bottom left*) The *Altmark* passes herself off as the *Chiriqui*—one of her disguises

(*Above right*) The bankbook that became a log of the voyage (*Fotopress, Dundee*)

(*Right*) A section of the log kept by Melville-Evans (*Fotopress, Dundee*)

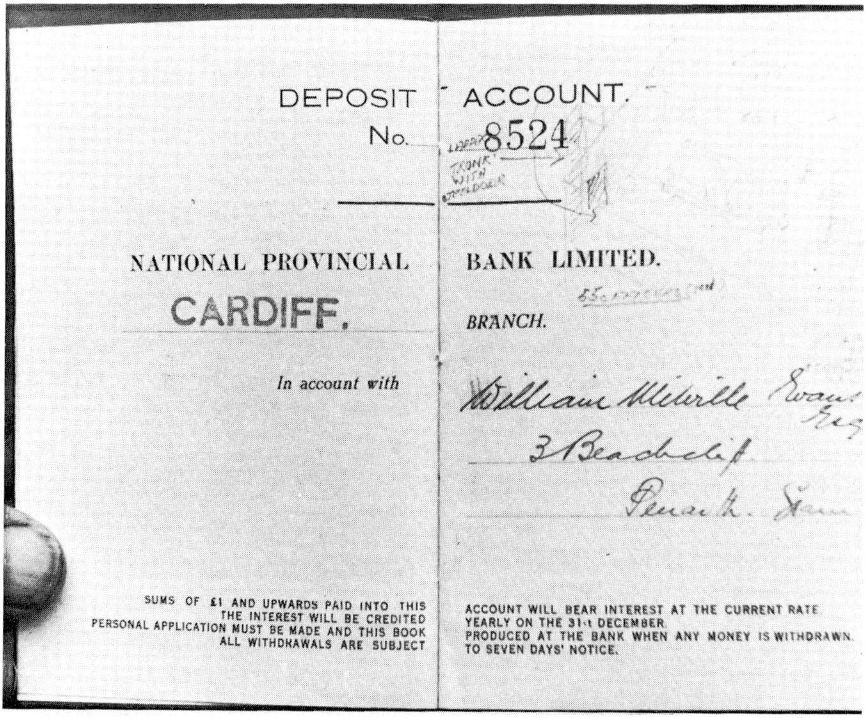

DEPOSIT ACCOUNT.

No. 8524

NATIONAL PROVINCIAL BANK LIMITED.

CARDIFF. BRANCH.

In account with William Melville Evans Esq

3 Beachcliff

Penarth. Glam

SUMS OF £1 AND UPWARDS PAID INTO THIS ACCOUNT WILL BEAR INTEREST AT THE CURRENT RATE. THE INTEREST WILL BE CREDITED YEARLY ON THE 31st DECEMBER. PERSONAL APPLICATION MUST BE MADE AND THIS BOOK PRODUCED AT THE BANK WHEN ANY MONEY IS WITHDRAWN. ALL WITHDRAWALS ARE SUBJECT TO SEVEN DAYS' NOTICE.

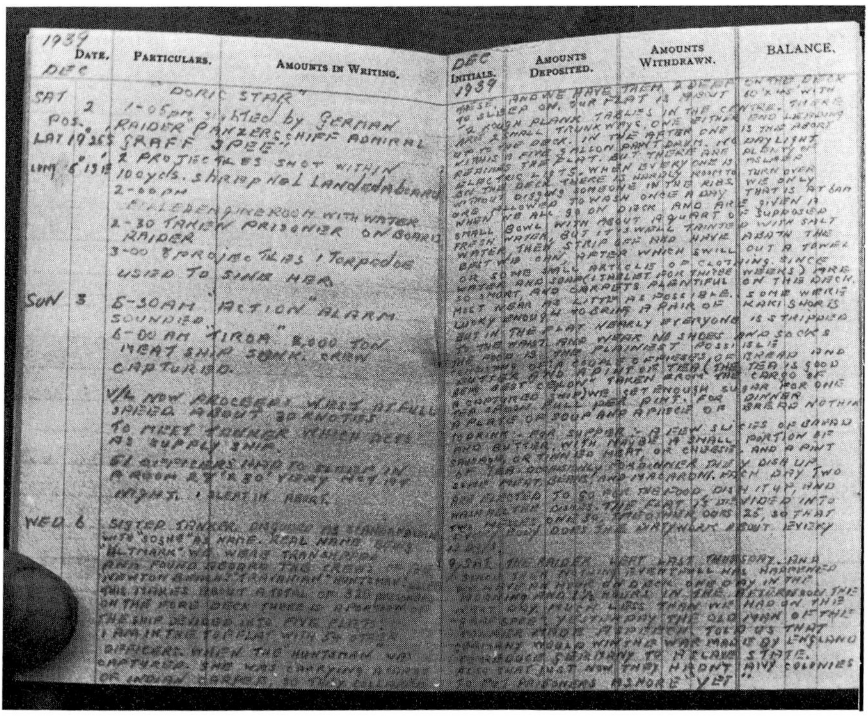

1939 DEC

Date.		Particulars.	Amounts in Writing.
		"DORIC STAR"	
SAT	2	1-05pm sighted by German Raider "Panzerschiff Admiral Graff Spee"	
POS. LAT 19°26'S LONG 5°13'E		2 projectiles shot within 100yds. shrapnel landed aboard	
		2-00pm Flooded engine room with water	
		2-30 Taken prisoner on board raider	
		3-00 [illegible] projectiles 1 torpedo used to sink her.	
SUN	3	5-30AM "Action" alarm sounded.	
		6-00AM "Tiroa" 8,000 ton meat ship sunk. crew captured.	
		V/L now proceeds west at full speed about 30 knots to meet [illegible] which acts as supply ship.	
		61 officers had to sleep in a room 25' x 30' very hot at night. I slept in [illegible].	
WED	6	Sister tanker. [illegible] with "SOSHE" as name. Real name being "Altmark" we were transhipped and found aboard the crews of the Newton Beech, "Trairhiam", "Huntsman". This makes about a total of 3[illegible] prisoners. On the [illegible] deck there is a portion of the ship divided into five flats. I am in the top flat with 54 other officers. When the Huntsman was captured she was carrying [illegible] of Indian [illegible]	

DEC Initials. 1939	Amounts Deposited.	Amounts Withdrawn.	Balance.
[illegible], and we have them 2 deep on the deck to sleep on. Our flat is about 60' x 45' with [illegible] plank tables in the centre. There are 2 small trunkways, one either end leading up to the deck. In the after one is the abort [illegible] is five gallon paint drum. No daylight reaches the flat, but there are plenty of electric lights. When everyone is [illegible] on the deck there is hardly room to turn over without digging someone in the ribs. We only are allowed to wash once a day, that is at 6am when we all go on deck and are given a small bowl with about a quart of supposed fresh water, but it is usually tainted with salt water. Then strip off and have a bath. The best we can after which [illegible] out a towel or some small articles of clothing. Since water and soap [illegible] for three weeks) are so short, and carpets plentiful on the deck, [illegible] wear as little as possible. Some were lucky enough to bring a pair of khaki shorts but in the flat nearly everyone is stripped to the waist and wear no shoes and socks. The food is the plainest possible [illegible] of a couple of [illegible] of bread and butter and a pint of tea (the tea is good [illegible] taken from the cargo of a captured ship) we get enough sugar for one [illegible] per pint. For dinner a plate of soup and a piece of bread nothing to drink. For supper a few slices of bread and butter, with maybe a small portion of [illegible] or tinned meat or cheese, and a pint of tea. [illegible] for dinner they dish up [illegible] meat, beans and macaroni. Each day two are elected to go for the food, dish it up, and [illegible] the dishes. The flat is divided into [illegible] one 30, the other 25, so that [illegible] does the [illegible] about every [illegible] days.			
9 SAT. The raider left last Thursday, and since then nothing eventful has happened. We have an hour on deck one day in the morning and 1½ hours in the afternoon [illegible] much less than we had on the "Graff Spee". Yesterday the old man of the [illegible] told us that Germany would win the war made by England [illegible] Germany to a [illegible] state. Also that just now they hadn't any colonies to put prisoners ashore yet.			

The courageous *Cossack* shows a fine turn of speed (*Imperial War Museum*)

Vian of the *Cossack* with the rank of vice-admiral in 1946 (*Central Press Photos Ltd*)

Entering Jossingfjord protected by Norwegian torpedo-boats

The *Altmark* in Jossingfjord after the freeing of the prisoners. A Norwegian warship is in the background

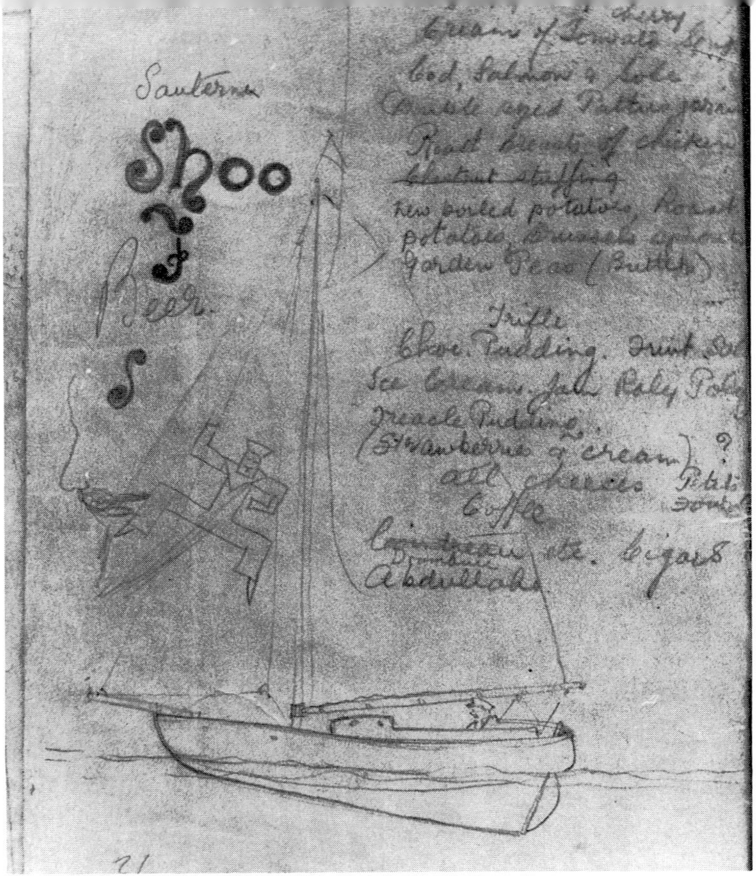

A ‘menu’ on the back of the secret chart (*Fotopress, Dundee*)

A pin-up sketched on the chart by Second Officer Archibald Willis (*Fotopress, Dundee*)

Becker had provided. But the messages just bobbed away in the tanker's wake, little dots in an endless ocean and with only a remote chance of being picked up.

The weather was becoming warmer now as the *Altmark* left the desolate regions of the Southern Ocean. Dau gave orders that the prisoners were to be allowed on deck for 50 minutes every other day. Melville-Evans, Willis and Wally Wells strolled along the deck at exercise time and discussed their prospects.

"It's good to see the sun again," said Melville-Evans as they gazed about them and looked for any unusual signs of activity among the tanker's crew. There was nothing to indicate anything unusual. Dau was on the bridge with Paulsen, and members of the crew were busy cleaning the decks after the mess caused by the overhauling of the engines. Willis was wishing he could sketch the scene and the blue sea beyond the tanker's bows. The wind was whipping up white caps and there was a sense of peace over everything.

"It looks like she's escaped the Dakar patrol," commented Wells as he scanned the ocean, empty with not a sign of life as far as the horizon. "Our only hope is the home patrol. If she gets past that, then we'll end up in a prison camp for sure. Dau's had all the luck so far."

"Don't be so sure," Willis broke in. "They're scared stiff. Look at the lookouts they've got. Dau's like a cat on hot bricks, and Babyface and the guards are not too happy. They realize we are reaching a crucial time. Tyrolt was only talking this morning of the chances of getting through, but Babyface shut him up just when it seemed he might give something away."

"Still, we've got the beggars tracked," commented Melville-Evans as he put his right hand to his eyes and scanned the sea. "We're managing to get a rough position nearly every day, and in nine days' time we expect to be just north of Iceland. We are not doing so badly with the sights, seeing our navigation is all done through a ventilator."

The others agreed. It was also lucky, they thought, that the *Doric Star*'s "third" had managed to keep the chart with him after being taken aboard the *Graf Spee*. "A stroke of luck that, Mel," Willis said as they moved into line to go below decks again.

Noon found the "navigating team" busily at work taking sights. "We're making good progress," said Melville-Evans as he marked off the chart. "Not far to Iceland now."

Suddenly there was a warning hiss as boots clattered on the trunkway ladder. Dau stepped into the flat just as Melville-Evans turned over the chart so that all that could be seen were sketches of semi-nudes on the other side.

"Well, gentlemen, how are we today?" Dau seemed in jovial mood. Things were going well at the moment. The *Altmark* was making good progress and they had not been spotted. His hopes of reaching home safely were rising each day.

His roving gaze spotted the chart, which Melville-Evans was trying discreetly to hide. "What is this?" he said, pointing at the chart. He moved across the flat while the Merchant Navy officers held their breath in suspense. It looked as if the game was up, and that Dau was to win yet another round after the thwarting of their message attempts.

Dau leaned forward but did not pick up the chart. His eyes were held by the drawings. "Who did these?" he asked, gazing at Melville-Evans. "Not me," said the *Doric Star*'s third officer, wondering at the same time what Dau was up to.

"I did," volunteered Willis. "It gives me something to do and entertains the chaps. After all, we haven't seen a woman in months." He laughed as he turned his gaze to the scantily clad female forms he had sketched on the back of the chart.

"Excellent, excellent," commented Dau. "You would do well to consider taking this work up after the war," he advised before passing on to inspect the rest of the flat, followed by Otto Schmidt, who was glad that Dau was in a good mood for his inspection of the prisoners' quarters. He had a certain awe of the *Altmark*'s captain. He was a different type from the kind Langsdorff had been. Both were men of the old school, but whereas Langsdorff had been a gentleman, Dau was one of those who had come up the hard way in merchant vessels. It was also apparent that he had no great love for the British. It was a surprise to find him in pleasant mood as he made the rounds.

"Phew, that was a close shave," said Smith of the *Tairoa*. "Thought it was all up that time. Good job the old devil seems in a good mood. If he hadn't been, he could easily have had that chart in his hands and then the fat would have been in the fire. We'll have to watch it in future."

"He might have seen what we were up to had he had a closer look and started reading the 'menus'", said Willis.

This was a reference to the habit they had fallen into of planning menus of meals they would like whenever they got the chance again. After finishing their meagre supper of bread and butter, with a piece of sausage or tinned meat, they would settle down to discuss their ideal meal.

"What are you ordering tonight?" someone would ask, and then the "ordering" of dishes that had to remain in their imagination would begin.

"I'll have fruit juice for starters," Willis would say, making a note on the back of the chart.

"I think I would like salmon, with treacle pudding for dessert," Melville-Evans liked to put in as names of dishes were shouted out.

Wally Wells preferred ice cream to finish with, and Smith wanted new potatoes and chicken. Mouths watered, too, at the thought of trifle and ice cream. And from all of them there was a demand for coffee, cigars and liqueurs to round off the meal.

The chart with its list of inviting dishes would then be put aside for another time while the men discussed meals they had enjoyed. It was significant that while they had all enjoyed exotic dishes in various parts of the world, they all chose something so typically English as chicken and treacle pudding when selecting their "meals". It was a reminder of English hotels, country inns and meals they had eaten in their own homes.

The planning of menus helped to relieve the monotony of life in the flats. Some promised themselves they would one day enjoy meals like those they had "ordered", but realized that even if they got home, there was little chance of wartime Britain being able to serve up meals that belonged to peacetime tables. But it all provided an escape from life in the *Altmark*, and escape was what they wanted. Yet would they ever escape from this ship that seemed to elude the whole might of the Royal Navy? Time was getting short.

7

Land at Last

The *Altmark* officers, with the exception of those on watch, were once again assembled in Dau's cabin. Dau, aware that the time of maximum danger was approaching, had called them together to ask their views on what they considered to be the best route for the last leg of the voyage.

"Gentlemen," he said, pointing to the chart spread out before him, "I am concerned as to what route we should take to have the greatest chance of avoiding the British patrols. We have come thus far without being seen, but now we are approaching the shipping routes and the British will be doubly alert. It would be a pity to be caught at the last moment. We have speed, but if destroyers or cruisers see us, then we have no chance. We can only surrender, and so bring an inglorious end to our cruise.

"I would like your opinion on what you consider is our best route. It is my view that we should set course through the western North Atlantic, then through the Shetland Islands to Norway. What do you think?"

This time there was a pause as the officers considered Dau's proposal. How different he sounded now compared with his madcap scheme to attack Cape Town. He was obviously as anxious as they were to get home.

The merits and otherwise of the plan were considered. Finally, it was decided that the route should be between Iceland and the Faroe Islands, sailing some fifteen to twenty miles south of the south coast of Iceland.

"It will be the time of the new moon, Herr Kapitaen," Paulsen pointed out. "There is also the chance that we shall run into fog, wind and rain and not be seen by the British patrols. But we shall need a lot of luck."

"I agree," said Walter Schmidt. "We have a good chance sailing by that route." Garte and de Harde were of the same view. It seemed to them that keeping close to the Icelandic coast would afford them better protection against being spotted.

"If that is your considered view, gentlemen, then we sail by Iceland. Paulsen, see that the necessary charts are to hand," said Dau as he prepared to go to the bridge again.

Coded messages continued to arrive from S.K.L. in Berlin, but the *Altmark* maintained radio silence. For their part, S.K.L. had no idea of the *Altmark*'s position, or whether indeed she was still at liberty.

The beat of the engines told those in the flats that the *Altmark* was still steaming steadily. The captives noticed when allowed on deck for exercise that there was an even greater degree of watchfulness among the crew than usual. There was an air of tension, too, and the guards were more brusque as they ordered the prisoners about. Dau could be seen pacing the bridge and snapping out orders. Even the cook and the carpenter seemed subdued whenever they were near the prisoners.

The carpenter, Becker, when questioned, said: "We are going home and do not want your British Navy to spot us. It could also be bad for you if they start shooting. We have no time to save you if the shells start falling. It is better for all if your ships do not spot us. At least you will be safe if we get back to Germany."

"You can keep that," shouted several of the men who had been listening. "We'll take our chance with the Navy. They know we're aboard and will not shell us."

"They've got to find us first," put in Wally Wells as the men turned into the flats and prepared for yet more games with which to amuse themselves.

Games and discussions filled in a lot of the time. One of the difficulties in discussions was in getting a definite ruling on the subject being discussed. It was then that a 1930 edition of *Pears Encyclopaedia* in the possession of a member of the crew of the *Ashlea* came in useful. This treasured copy seldom let them down.

The question: "What can we do tonight?" would sometimes bring the reply: "Let's have a mock wedding." Then they would rummage through their scanty wardrobe and dress the "bride and groom". The bizarre-looking couple would then draw roars of laughter from the "congregation". It was all harmless fun, as were the wrestling matches held between the various departments of the different ships or companies represented.

The prisoners were particularly fond of a game they called "Pile-on". If for any reason someone had offended the rest of the deck, say for serving up food unevenly or letting his partner down at cards, the culprit would be lured to a suitable part of the deck and brought down by a mass attack. The result was a seething mass of bodies. It did not matter if the original culprit wriggled free or not, as everybody just went on piling on top of the nearest man to him until the crowd were either too exhausted to carry on, or the heat and dust became too much.

Cigarettes and tobacco continued to be a problem. Many men were now without any. Cigarette ends—what few there were—became like gold, being unpicked and remade into new cigarettes.

When these ran out, tea leaves were dried out and mixed with what tobacco was left. Toilet paper was used in place of cigarette papers. The end result tasted vile, but it was a "smoke" for men who were desperate for a decent cigarette and tobacco.

The tea-leaf smokes were endured for a few weeks until it was discovered that the Lascars were in the habit of taking quite a lot of tobacco with them whenever they went to England. This they had with them in the *Altmark* and after a lot of hard bargaining the prisoners were able to reach agreement over prices. The price went as high as thirty shillings a pound, but a lot changed hands for clothing.

It did not take long, however, for this source of supply to be exhausted, and it was back to tea leaves again. The flats reeked of the acrid fumes as men tried to seek what solace they could from this substitute for tobacco. The non-smokers were the ones who enjoyed freedom from the craving, but they had to suffer the smoke and fumes as the smokers continued their experiments with substitute tobacco. It was a trying time and nerves became under more strain as the *Altmark* drove closer and closer to Iceland.

Escape or rescue continued to be uppermost in the thoughts of the captives. Now the *Altmark* was heading for Iceland there was even more talk of trying to take over the ship. The young ones were for making a dash for the bridge, overpowering the navigating officers and then fanning out over the vessel armed with what weapons they could seize from the guards.

"I don't think we should risk losing our lives in this way. Have you forgotten that our only exit from these flats is covered by the machine guns on the bridge?" said Willis as the officers discussed taking over the ship.

The exit was also guarded by two armed men. There was also the fact that any rush for the bridge would probably result in the deaths of the men who would have been responsible for the running of the *Altmark* once she was seized. There would have been little chance of those remaining getting the full co-operation of Dau and his officers in navigating the *Altmark*. It was probable, too, that the Germans, with few British officers surviving, would have been able to hoodwink the remaining captives as to the actual course. It was also possible that in such circumstances the *Altmark* might risk breaking radio silence and send a message to S.K.L. as the takeover was attempted.

It would then be easy to divert a U-boat from patrol to intercept the *Altmark*. They could then surrender to the U-boat as she trained her gun on the tanker, or risk a torpedo. Wally Wells did not think a U-boat commander would have too many scruples about sinking the *Altmark* if that was the only way she could be overcome.

The arguments raged in all the flats. Some of the schemes were so useless or ridiculous that they were thrown out before even being discussed. Wiser heads prevailed, and there was also the deciding factor that whatever the faults, there was no driving force in the form of starvation or brutality. Men were not being beaten or starved. A few days in the "cooler" for smoking in a restricted area could hardly be called brutality. Dau might shout and threaten and cut rations, but that was as far as it went.

"I don't see any point in us risking our lives for something that hasn't much chance of succeeding," said Smith, the *Tairoa* chief steward, as he listened to yet another scheme that could only have come out of a Hollywood film, with someone like Clark Gable or Gary Cooper rushing the bridge in a death or glory dash under a hail of bullets.

"I reckon," put in Smith, "that sooner or later the Navy is bound to show up. They've lost us for the time being, I admit, but as we get nearer Iceland we stand a good chance of running into a patrol. I think our best chance is to forget about rushing the bridge and think about organizing ourselves to make a break when we get a real chance. We can keep watch at the hatches and then try to attract attention if we get near another ship or the coast."

"I think he's got something there," said Melville-Evans. "We don't want to end up dead ducks. Those machine-guns look nasty pieces of work, and I don't fancy playing the hero. Let's be ready to attract attention whenever we get the chance. We have our whistles, and we can blow like mad on them if a ship comes close or *Altmark* enters harbour."

The men broke up, feeling that at least they had got something on which to build, even if some of the younger ones still nursed a desire to "have a crack" at the Germans. It was also agreed that, in the meantime, any opportunities of getting a message overboard should be taken.

One idea for getting a message away was a proposal to use a contraceptive. If they could produce hydrogen, which one engineer claimed he could, given the necessary materials, the contraceptive could be inflated with this. It could then be released into the air with a message tied to the end of it. The contraceptive would have to be released under cover of darkness. The plan never reached fruition, like so many others that were put forward, but it all helped to pass the time and gave the men something to think about.

It was also becoming obvious that sooner or later they were going to reach the Norwegian coast. As the *Altmark* would then be close to land, and perhaps quite close on some occasions, it would afford a chance of someone slipping overboard and swimming for the shore.

The idea put forward was that a volunteer should conceal himself on deck, hide until dark, grease himself all over and then slip over the side and make for land as the *Altmark* hugged the coast. It was another scheme that did not get off the ground. When the men considered the icy conditions the swimmer would encounter, enthusiasm for the plan waned.

Melville-Evans, who enjoyed swimming, debated the merits of the scheme to himself then suddenly thought, "My God, this is icy water." A man could get into difficulties in minutes in a sea like that. The current could also sweep him along the coast instead of on to it. If he did reach the shore, what could a man, naked and exhausted, do? He would have to struggle to a village, and then make himself understood. There was no guarantee that even then the men held prisoner in the *Altmark* would be saved. The odds were that the whole episode would end with the swimmer losing his life after surviving so long as a prisoner. It would all have been in vain.

It was the general feeling that now they had come so far, they should take no unnecessary risks. They had survived the sinking of their ships, had kept reasonably fit despite the cramped conditions and poor food, and it was felt it would be futile to risk loss of life in any venture that was probably doomed to failure from the start.

There was little to do but to occupy themselves as best they could.

Men turned again to their diaries to record the events of the days that passed by, each one much like the other.

Melville-Evans noted on 10th February:

> Here is the tenth week and we are now approaching England and the hoped for blockade. This week has been fairly quiet except for a three-day gale, which did everything but turn us over. If, by next Wednesday, there is no entry in this book, then I'm afraid our stay as Hitler's unwilling guests will be prolonged until Hitler isn't. Still our confidence in the Navy will stand until then.

There was a stir in the flats when it was learned that the tanker's name had been changed back to *Altmark*, and that her colour had reverted to a black and grey hull, grey funnel and white deckhouses. She was now the same colour as when she had sailed from Germany the previous August.

"What do you make of it?" asked Wally Wells as the officers' flat buzzed with speculation. "I'd say she was preparing for the time when she is stopped when she gets to Norway," said one officer.

"*If* she gets to Norway," put in Melville-Evans. "But it does seem as if she is expecting to beat the blockade," he was forced to concede.

The crew of the *Altmark* were not so confident as Melville-Evans was inclined to think. Dau was, in fact, a worried man. The gale that had blown for three days had been trouble enough when standing watch. It had also made conditions uncomfortable for the crew as well as for the prisoners. The one consolation had been that the gale also made them less vulnerable to the enemy, who would have had difficulties in coping with the weather.

Dau was concentrating on keeping his ship on course, and on making as much speed as possible as huge waves lashed the ship. The balmy days and warmth of the South Atlantic were things of the past, although there had been bitter weather while hiding in the Southern Ocean wastes.

S.K.L. had sent a message in code ordering Dau to enter Norwegian waters north of 61° latitude because German submarines had orders to attack all tankers sailing south of this latitude. Langsdorff had decreed that the homeward-bound course for both the *Graf Spee* and the *Altmark* should be in the area of Dakar and then to the Shetlands before making the final dash for Germany. If these arrangements failed, then the *Graf Spee* and *Altmark* were to set separate courses for home. The loss of the pocket battleship left Dau with no alternative but to set a lone course.

The *Altmark* was now close to Iceland. There had been two narrow escapes when the lookouts had reported vessels. Dau had ordered a swift change of course to avoid being identified by the vessels, which were seen to be trawlers fishing. The crews of the trawlers had apparently not spotted the *Altmark*, or at least had given no sign of having done so.

It was 10th February and the tanker was running at full revolutions, the M.A.N. diesels driving her nearer and nearer her destination. Every eye was straining towards the horizon, seeking any sign that danger was close.

Suddenly, Dau, on the bridge that he now seldom left, looked up, alerted by the buzz of the bridge telephone. He snatched it up: "One light, 30 degrees on the port side, Herr Kapitaen," came the voice of the lookout on the forecastle. "Starboard five by five degrees," barked Dau. He ordered the chief engineer to reduce speed so that the funnel gave out no tell-tale sparks and also so that noise would be reduced.

It was then one hour after midnight. It was dark, but with good visibility and a cold wind blowing. Nerves were strained to breaking point as Dau gave orders to be ready to destroy the sea-valves if the other ship gave any indication of having seen them.

The light had gone out and Dau guessed that it was caused by the glow of a cigarette held by a careless sailor trying to snatch a surreptitious smoke. When the other vessel was abeam, the watchers in the *Altmark* could make out the silhouette of a large warship, westbound and two to three miles away.

"Go on the poop-deck and report all movements of that vessel," Dau ordered Third Officer Schmidt. "She may have seen us, and we must be ready in case she has," he added.

Crew members took up their stations in readiness for burning the ship and for opening the sea-valves. Preparations were also made for the release of the prisoners, half to go to the forecastle and the rest to the poop-deck. Then Schmidt noticed that the warship, of unknown nationality, was turning away and immediately informed Dau. "Another lucky escape," exclaimed Dau as he nervously fingered his goatee. "We have been lucky so far, but we cannot depend on our luck holding. We must be alert all the time."

"What was all that about?" said Willis as he and the others noticed the reduction in speed. There had also been activity outside the hatches.

"I don't know. They must have seen something to cut speed," said Melville-Evans. "She has been going to full speed until now. It might be the Navy. It's time they put in an appearance."

"Listen!" Willis held up his hand. "The ship's increasing speed again and all seems to have gone quiet on deck. Whatever the danger was, it must now be over."

"Well," said Smith, "if the Navy don't do something soon, we can get used to the idea of ending up in a German prison camp. And you can bet that the guards won't be like this lot here. They will also be different from Tyrolt. We were talking to him only this morning and laughing as he tried to pick up more English."

The officers settled down again for what was left of the night. But sleep came only fitfully as men wondered what lay ahead of them in the next few days. Melville-Evans thought of his family in South Wales. He had managed to remain fairly fit despite the conditions, and plotting the course of the *Altmark* had also helped to keep his mind active. They had observed the Germans taking sights at noon, and he was reasonably confident that they were keeping an accurate shadow check of the *Altmark*'s course. Either way, they would not be keeping track for long, he reflected.

It was now becoming clear that if there was to be any chance of escape it must come within the next few days. For the hundredth time, the prisoners discussed what they would do if the opportunity for escape arose.

The large trunkway at the after end of the prisoners' decks was divided into two by a bulkhead through its centre. These two exits, along with the small trunkway at the forward end, gave each of the three prison decks a separate means of exit. It was agreed that in the event of any attempt at escape, the lowest deck should use the forward trunkway, the middle deck the port side of the large trunkway, and the top deck the starboard side. By this means, there would be as little confusion as possible and all should be able to get on deck quickly.

That was all very well, but there still remained a major problem—how to break open the door and hatch covers? The answer was not long in coming. For storing ammunition, all five decks were fitted with a removable system of racks made from steel stanchions and cross-pieces. All the racks had been dismantled before the captives moved in and the parts were stored at one end of each deck. The prisoners chose the most useful items from these and placed them in readiness near the doors.

It was decided that as the officers occupied the top deck, they should organize everything and also maintain all lookouts and direct any attempt that was to be made. In the top deck, a system of lookouts was arranged that ensured there were two men on duty every hour. If they had anything to report, it was to be passed down by word of mouth to the lower decks, so that all would have a "running commentary" on what was happening. It was planning that was to pay dividends in the days ahead.

The Germans were also preparing for what lay ahead. Dau wanted them to be viewed as just a harmless tanker. She had her own identity again, but there was still another important task to be done before the *Altmark* could appear wholly innocent. The guns and anti-aircraft guns had to be removed. These were stowed part by part in concealed storerooms, so that the *Altmark*, still one day away from the Norwegian coast, became, to the casual observer, an unarmed supply ship of the German Navy. She also flew a special Reich Service flag. It was this guise as an unarmed supply ship that was to add to the bone of contention when warships of neutral Norway became involved. Dau hoped that his bluff would work.

Dau called his officers together for another conference. He gazed around the cabin at them.

"Well, gentlemen, it won't be long now before we reach Norway," he began. "It will be a time of great danger. Remember, once we reach the Norwegian coast, we shall no doubt be halted by the Norwegians. They are not at war with us, and they will be anxious to protect their neutrality. I don't think they will want to risk an incident, but neither will they be easily fooled.

"We have hidden the guns, but we can only keep the prisoners in their quarters. We must not let the Norwegians know they are on board. If they stop us and want to search the ship, then it will be difficult for us. We must try by all means to keep any Norwegians who board us on the bridge or deck. They must not be allowed to make a proper search, and we must also see that any noise the prisoners make to attract attention is not heard by the Norwegians. We have come this far, and I do not want us to fail at the last moment. I want to see the Britishers delivered to a German prisoner-of-war camp," he stated.

Dau was well aware that the prisoners were entitled to release once the *Altmark* entered Norwegian territorial waters. He did not dwell on this point. He considered them prisoners of war and was determined to reach Germany with them. There was no question of handing them over to the Norwegians.

"If we are careful," he continued, "there is no reason why we should not pass as a normal German supply ship. It is the British we must watch for. They do not know where we are, but they know that if they do not catch us off Norway, then we have a good chance of reaching Germany safely."

"That would be fine, Herr Kapitaen," put in Chief Officer Paulsen. "We have been away so long. We have not touched land since leaving America last August. I hope we can reach the Fatherland without any more trouble."

Third Officer Schmidt hoped so, too. He had not seen his young bride, Lilly, for so long, and at times he had thought he would never seen her again. Now they were almost home—if they could bluff the Norwegians. The Norwegians had no particular reason to be friendly towards the Germans. It was going to need all the luck they could get.

First Engineer Schleusner was hoping that he would have no trouble with the engines. They had served them well since the overhaul in the South Atlantic and he did not want any hitches at this late stage. The cook, Schwill, and the baker, Treibel, were tired of making do with dwindling supplies.

"If we get back to Germany, I will bake a big cake to celebrate," said Treibel. Schwill promised he would help cook a big meal for the crew once they were home. Both men knew that their banter was a cover for their fears. Great danger lay ahead. If they fooled the Norwegians, they still had to contend with the British Navy. The Tommies had beaten the *Graf Spee*. What could their *Altmark* do against their warships?

"No use worrying," said Schwill as he began to prepare another meal. "We must hope that all goes well." Treibel nodded in agreement, thinking that he did not really care about baking a cake so long as they reached home.

In the officers' flat, the dreaming up of delectable menus had long since ceased as the men waited for every report from the watchers at the spyholes. The chart was still being kept, and it was obvious that they were to make landfall soon.

Otto Schmidt was not now so forthcoming with the prisoners. For months he and his guards had had the upper hand over the captives. There had been a lot of banter between them, but that had been in the days of comparative safety. Now anything could happen if the prisoners thought they had a chance of freedom. He did not want to do any shooting unless circumstances compelled drastic action. He began to wonder whether he would not have been better off in the *Graf Spee*.

Dr Tyrolt was still his cheerful self. "Nothing seems to get that chap down," commented Melville-Evans as the doctor made another of his morning rounds and chatted with the prisoners, most of whom had forgotten their minor aches and pains as they waited for something to happen, though what they were not quite sure.

Cigarettes began to appear here and there. Some men had secreted some for just such an occasion as this, and now they drew on them nervously as the hours slipped by. Others made do with the usual mixture of tea leaves and toilet paper.

The men sang songs to keep up their spirits and to show that they were not down-hearted. Yet beneath the stiff-upper-lip approach and japes that were reminiscent of boys' magazine stories, there was an underlying anxiety. Men often got on each other's nerves in the confines of the flats. There was also the degrading business of using the sawn-off drums that passed for lavatories. The smell was foul and in warmer conditions there would have been a danger of disease breaking out. Men, as they wiped themselves down with wet cloths as best they could, dreamed of hot baths.

The simple things of life they had taken for granted for so long—proper toilets, hot baths, decent meals—now began to take on great importance in their thoughts as hopes of freedom grew. The mere pleasure of turning on a tap and seeing hot water pouring from it would be something to be savoured whenever they were free. It would be pleasant to sit down at a table with a clean cloth and enjoy a decent meal, and to round off the day by slipping between clean sheets for a good night's rest. It would be pleasant, too, to walk along a road or across a field and stretch one's legs.

The confined conditions were taking their toll on some of the men. They would doze fitfully, dreaming of home, of a wife or girlfriend, or of some pleasant incident in the past, only to awake and find themselves staring at the steel bulkhead. It was hard for some of them to keep up their hopes. They had been so full of hope after learning of the end of the *Graf Spee* and been confident that it would not be long before the Navy freed them.

Now the weeks had passed without a sign of the Navy. Men, even those of the strongest of character, must have some hope to which to cling if they are to survive in adverse conditions. Men in prison camps in all wars have kept up their hopes that the next day would bring some relief; that a new dawn would see an end to their suffering.

Escape! The magic word that men held captive cling to as day follows day. But how do you escape from a ship in the middle of an ocean whose crew, or at least some of them, are determined that there shall be no escape; that their duty is to deliver you into yet another prison? The monotony, the uncertainty, the plain and unchanging food, and the cramped living conditions had become greater enemies than the Germans, who were at least also suffering, though in not quite the same way.

Wednesday, 14th February dawned. It was a day the prisoners would never forget. Land was sighted. The *Altmark* had reached Norway. The hunted and the hunters were soon to meet.

8

Inspect the *Altmark*

While the *Altmark* to all intents and purposes seemed to have vanished without trace, she still remained a source of concern to the Norwegians. The Germans wanted her safely back in Germany and the British wanted her captured, but the Norwegians were concerned in another respect. The Norwegian newspaper *Aftenposten* reported in January that the *Altmark* was trying to reach home across the Atlantic, and that when last seen was bearing the name *Sogne*, with Oslo as her port of registration. This news caused the Officer Commanding the 2nd Naval Defence District, Rear-Admiral C. Tank-Nielsen, to draw the conclusion that the *Altmark* would try to pass through Norwegian waters in her bid to get back to Germany. He ordered that he was to receive at once any information about the tanker.

The news of the *Altmark* was also a reminder of another incident involving a German ship, the *Westerwald*, a tanker similar to the *Altmark*. This had occurred in November 1939. The captain had refused to have his vessel searched. He sought refuge under the state flag, the Reichsdienstflagge. This was the flag carried by ships in the service of the state as opposed to warships.

The captain's refusal to have his vessel—classed as an auxiliary ship belonging to the German Navy—searched caused a flutter in diplomatic circles. It was the German view that as the ship was in the service of the state it was not necessary for her master to agree to examination. The tanker was accordingly allowed to proceed through territorial waters until she reached the Bergen Defended Area, where there was more confusion.

More discussions took place, but in the end the *Westerwald* was allowed to sail through the area under escort. The Norwegian Minister of Foreign Affairs, Dr Halvdan Koht, stated in a letter to the Norwegian Ministry of Defence that such dispensation allowing passage through a defended area should not be allowed again.

The fact remained, however, that a precedent involving Norwegian neutrality regulations had now been set. No one could have guessed at that stage that the same sort of problem was to arise again within a short time and to involve a vessel that was also in the service of the German State. None could have guessed either that this time she would not be sailing unnoticed, but would have the British Navy hunting her and determined to capture her if at all possible.

It was twenty minutes short of four o'clock on the morning of 14th February 1940, when the *Altmark* made her presence known to the world again and caused wires to start humming. It was the start of what promised to be just another routine day at Linesoy coastguard station on Fosen until the tanker came into view. The *Altmark* sailed into territorial waters close to Halten, north of Trondheimsfjord. Her arrival began a train of events that were to have repercussions in Oslo, London and Berlin and to arouse controversy in years to come.

The first news that the *Altmark* had reached the Norwegian coast was brought to the officer-prisoners by the two men whose duty it was to empty the lavatory drum overboard that day. One of them was Wally Wells. The seventh engineer of the *Tairoa* and the other prisoners had spent an anxious night expecting the *Altmark* to be mined or torpedoed at any minute. It was a relief, therefore, when, at 6.30 a.m., Wally Wells and his companion were called on deck to empty the drum, for what was to prove to be the last time this duty was performed.

There it was—the Norwegian coast in the red glow of a glorious sunrise. It was a magnificent sight for men who had not seen land for months. They clattered back down into the flats shouting: "Land! We've seen land. It's Norway." There was great excitement. This was it. Surely they would be rescued now, and the *Altmark* was bound to be stopped and searched by the Norwegians. "It won't be long now, lads," said Wells. "The Navy can't be far away, and, in any case, the Norwegians aren't going to let Dau go through. The whole world will know within a short time that the *Altmark* is sailing off Norway. The Navy will act. They'll get us out of this, even if the Norwegians don't act before." His was a simple faith that knew nothing of diplomatic manoeuvres and neutrality regulations.

Only a few of those in the officers' flat had sailed in Norwegian waters. There was conjecture as to where they actually were as they could not get a clear idea from what little they could observe through their spyhole in the small escape hatch door. The foredeck and the sea on the port side could be seen, but that was all. The eight-foot-square hatch had a wooden grille over it with a canvas cover over that. This could be lifted slightly to enable one man to perch precariously at the top of the hatch and see both the port and starboard sides of the foredeck. These vantage spots were to prove invaluable for watching ships' movements in the tense hours that lay ahead.

"It's a glorious view, if nothing else," said Willis as he took a turn at the observation points. His artistic eye took in the steep, snow-covered shore, with here and there fishing villages right on the water's edge. Numerous fishing boats were seen and a few freighters. Hopes ran high that British agents would see and recognize the *Altmark* and pass the word to Britain.

It was estimated that the *Altmark*, sailing inside the fjords, was moving at some 8 knots. At dusk, she arrived outside what, to the prisoners, seemed to be a large harbour. The *Altmark* was manoeuvred inside the breakwater and appeared to be moving alongside a wharf. It was difficult for the captives to see any clear details because of the limitations of their view and because of the darkness. It was the general opinion that the *Altmark* had interned herself.

The flats were agog with speculation, and it was decided that they must try to attract the attention of the Norwegians. A sing-song was started and iron bars, ready to hand, were thumped against the deckhead. The Germans reacted by starting up the steam-winches and putting out all the lights, leaving the prisoners to settle down for the night in darkness. This did not prevent the captives from setting watches and drawing a rough sketch of the harbour, which they believed to be on the mouth of Sognefjord.

The impression gathered by the British Merchant Navy officers and their men was confused, as was only to be expected. They were guessing most of the time, though they did well working within their limited resources.

The Germans were also not having things their own way, and a lot had been happening from the Norwegian aspect that neither the German crew nor the British prisoners knew anything about.

The Norwegian Naval authorities were keeping a close watch on the situation. The torpedo-boat *Trygg*, under the command of Lieutenant F. W. Munster, had actually made contact with *Altmark* during the afternoon following her arrival in Norwegian territorial waters. This she did in the Edoyfjord and an officer from the *Trygg* went aboard. Dau, who was on the bridge when the officer arrived, was anxious that no time be wasted and gave him what information he deemed wise without disclosing the *Altmark*'s true purpose.

Dau had to concede to himself that the Norwegians must be aware that the *Altmark* had been the supply vessel to the *Graf Spee* and that she was not just an innocent supply ship returning to Germany. He resorted to bluff, mixing half-truths and lies in his efforts to get his ship home now that they were not far from Germany. He told the officer that the tanker was on passage from Port Arthur to Germany with a cargo of fuel oil, with a crew of 133 and that she was not carrying any passengers. What he did not say was that while it was true the *Altmark* was carrying fuel oil, part of that cargo had been used to fuel the *Graf Spee* during her marauding in the South Atlantic.

The *Altmark* was flying the state flag, and Dau made great play of the fact that she was in the service of the state. He said he wanted a pilot and wished to sail along the coast to Kopervik, near Stavanger.

All the time Dau was on edge, but the Norwegian officer apparently found nothing to arouse his suspicions. There was no reason why he should, bearing in mind that the prisoners were safely locked in the holds. That the *Altmark* was a vessel in the service of the state also allayed any doubts he may have had about the fact that some of the crew wore German Naval uniforms. The officer noted the inspection in the *Altmark*'s log, returned to his own ship, and Dau was then given permission to proceed. Dau, now greatly relieved, also accepted the offer of the services of a pilot already on board *Trygg* to navigate the *Altmark* to Alesund.

There was a feeling of optimism in the flats. Men were packing their belongings—what few they had—in readiness for the freedom that they felt must now soon come. Some who had kept a few cigarettes back smoked them and said, "Well, it won't be long now before we get some more."

Conditions were becoming uncomfortable. The latrine drums remained unemptied and the air was stale. Men who tried to sleep—and few did—found themselves constantly awakened by the babble of voices from those who were too excited to sleep. "Babyface" Schmidt and his guards were tense. The least sound from outside was eagerly listened for, and when it came men tried to find a reason for it. Those at the observation holes were subjected to a barrage of "What's happening?", "What can you see?", and other questions as the prisoners waited for every scrap of news they could obtain.

Outside the air was crisp and clear, and the crew moved briskly to keep warm. Walter Schmidt gazed at the shore with its mantle of white, and at the Norwegian craft passing within hailing distance. It was a beautiful scene, he felt, if it had also not been so dangerous for the *Altmark*. He wondered how long Dau could go on bluffing the Norwegians. They had a long way to go yet before reaching Germany and safety. If they got through Norwegian waters, they would without a doubt have the British Navy to face. The British would pounce at the first opportunity. There would be both air and sea patrols looking for the *Altmark*.

If they were captured, then it would be a prison camp for the rest of the war for himself and the crew, Schmidt thought. If that happened, there was no knowing when he would see his wife again.

Dr Tyrolt had lost some of his cheerfulness. The conditions in the flats he had to admit were not good. The prisoners needed fresh air and exercise. Now it was out of the question. The last time he had made an inspection he had found the British in better health than he anticipated. There was, of course, the psychological fact that the prisoners were expecting to be freed shortly. This feeling was giving a boost to their spirits. They had stood up well to the conditions. A few months ago they had been sailing their ships in warm weather and enjoying the sunshine. The *Graf Spee* had put an end to all that.

Tyrolt was also worried that, if the prisoners should be freed as a result of a British attack, then the *Altmark* crew would be taken prisoner in their turn. He feared what the British would do to him, and had found little comfort in the assurances given to him by the prisoners.

"Don't worry, our chaps will treat you well," Wells had told the doctor when the question of the possible capture of the *Altmark* had been raised. "They won't cut off your hands and feet." He took comfort from that in what he knew were now to become the final desperate hours of the *Altmark*'s voyage. He had experienced many things in his full life, but his time in the *Altmark* looked like turning out to be the most exciting and dangerous of all.

Dau was concerned with more immediate events. He had successfully got out of one encounter. The officer from the *Trygg* had appeared to be satisfied, and had also accepted his explanation that the *Altmark* was armed with anti-aircraft guns, which had been removed before the vessel reached Norwegian waters. Everything seemed to be going well. If they could only remain free from interference from the Norwegians seeing that they had been inspected, there was a good chance of getting back to Germany. Langsdorff might have scuttled the *Graf Spee*, but he had no intention of doing the same with the

Altmark now that they had come so near their destination without too much difficulty.

Matters were not so simple as Dau hoped. One man at least was determined that the *Altmark* was not to have free rein while she was in Norwegian waters. Rear Admiral Tank-Nielsen gave instructions that the tanker was to have a Norwegian Navy escort throughout her period in territorial waters. He also ordered that another inspection be made of the *Altmark* as he was not satisfied with that carried out by the *Trygg*. The inspection was to be made when the *Altmark* reached Alesund in the evening. This time, the inspection was to be made by the torpedo-boat *Snogg*, in the command of Commander H. H. Simensen.

"What is this?" Dau exploded as he saw that the *Altmark* was to be boarded yet again. "Are the Norwegians not satisfied?" he asked anxiously of First Officer Paulsen as they watched the Norwegian officer coming aboard.

The result was the same. Dau gave the same facts as he had done when inspected by the *Trygg*. Dau was also concerned about sailing through the Bergen Defended Area, and was informed that he could only go through during daylight. Midnight was only half an hour away when the tanker set sail once again, this time with the intention of reaching Bergen by daybreak. The *Snogg* accompanied her as escort, which again caused Dau still more annoyance.

"I do not like this situation at all," he confided to Paulsen. "If this goes on, they are bound to discover that we have prisoners on board. We must do everything we can to drown any noise they make. Keep the winches going if they try to attract the Norwegians' attention. If they insist on making a proper search, then we are lost."

He glanced through the bridge windows and watched as the *Snogg* kept station on the *Altmark*. The Norwegians were certainly keeping them under close scrutiny, and matters were made worse when the *Snogg* was later joined by the destroyer *Draug*. The Norwegians seemed to be taking no chances.

"A torpedo-boat and a destroyer!" Dau exclaimed. "What do they think they are doing? We cannot escape. All we want is passage through these waters. One escort is surely sufficient." He turned in exasperation to Paulsen, who was watching the escorts through his glasses. "There is nothing we can do, I am afraid, Herr Kapitaen," he said. "So long as they do not search us, we have nothing to worry about." He sounded braver than he felt.

The inspections of the *Altmark* were not meeting with the approval of all in Norwegian official circles. The question of the *Altmark* being a state ship was raised, and there was surprise in one quarter at least that Dau had agreed to have his ship inspected.

Dau, for his part, would only permit the Norwegians to visit the quarters in the deckhouse, the bridge and the navigation room and to search for guns. The guns were well hidden in the storerooms. His main problem was that of keeping the presence of the prisoners concealed from the Norwegians. He knew that while the *Altmark* sailed in Norwegian waters, the prisoners were entitled to release. Dau wanted them in Germany and was going to do his best to see that they arrived there.

More delay faced Dau. There was to be yet another inspection. This was made by the *Snogg* in the Sognefjord, south of Steinsund, and again proved unsatisfactory. While the inspection was under way, there was bedlam in the prisoners' holds. The officers were blowing S.O.S. on their whistles and banging on the bulkheads with anything on which they could lay hands. The prisoners in the other flats were also going at it with iron bars and stamping and shouting. The noise was deafening, with the steam-winches being operated by the Germans making their contribution to the din. It seemed impossible that the Norwegians could be unaware of the commotion.

"It's no use, lads. The Norwegian boat is going back to the ship," the watcher at the small observation hole in the hatch door shouted down to the mêlée of men below him. Observation through the hatch cover had been obliterated as the Germans had secured the cover. The men sank down on the deck or on their makeshift beds too exhausted to do more than groan in dismay.

The officers considered their next move. Surely, they reasoned, the Norwegians, and certainly the pilots, must by now know that there was something suspicious about the *Altmark*. If they were not indeed suspicious, then why had they been stopped after the first inspection had appeared to satisfy them? There did not seem to be a satisfactory explanation.

"They're like policemen who keep returning to the scene of a crime," said Melville-Evans. "They get another clue and then they return to investigate it. Someone is not satisfied about this ship, otherwise we would have been on our way now without all this bother. Unless one of us can break out and dash on deck when, and if, the Norwegians board us again, I do not see how we are ever going to attract the Norwegians' attention at this rate." But he knew it was impossible for anyone to get on deck now that the Germans had secured the hatch.

The *Doric Star*'s third officer was more right than he knew when he said that someone among the Norwegians was not satisfied about the *Altmark*. That man was Rear-Admiral Tank-Nielsen, who read the report of the latest inspection and declared himself still not satisfied. There was only one thing to do—go and visit the *Altmark* himself.

Accordingly, he boarded the Norwegian destroyer *Garm*. It was also decided that Captain T. Stamso, acting chief of staff, 2nd Navy Defence District, would make the inspection. The admiral was determined that the question of the *Altmark* should be settled once and for all.

The case of the *Westerwald* hung like a spectre over the affair. Was the *Altmark* a merchant vessel or a warship? The question should soon be decided. Rear-Admiral Tank-Nielsen thought matters had gone far enough. The *Garm* sliced her way through the icy water, and another ray of hope was about to be raised for the prisoners in the *Altmark*.

The lookout saw a destroyer and heard the international code signal K, which means "I wish to communicate with you". It seemed that here at last was rescue and that the Norwegians could not fail to discover that the *Altmark* was carrying prisoners.

Those Germans who normally wore uniforms had hidden them, and were dressed as ordinary seamen, although they still carried their bayonets and revolvers under their jerseys. They had also started the steam-winches running to drown any noise coming from the prisoners' flats.

The destroyer moved in until she was only thirty to forty feet from the *Altmark*. Suddenly, the lookout at the hatch door shouted: "I can see her name! She's the *Garm*." Through the crack in the door, he could also see quite clearly the features of the crew on the *Garm*'s deck.

"Now!" shouted the lookout. The prisoners at once grabbed the pieces of steel from the ammunition racks in their quarters and attacked the two entrances to the prison, and almost succeeded in breaking out. The advantage was, however, with the Germans. They beat the prisoners back with pieces of board, steel bolts and hammers, and, finally, by forcing them down with hoses that sprayed icy jets of water on to them, soaking those who got in the way of the jets and generally making things uncomfortable in the captives' quarters.

Once again, it was bedlam. The winches were roaring away, the prisoners were shouting and singing and blowing S.O.S. on their whistles so that it was impossible for a man to make himself heard to the companion standing next to him.

To add to the confusion, the Germans put out the lights in the flats, but in spite of this the captives managed to get settled down and set about organizing their efforts better. The Germans were so worried about the presence of the captives being discovered, that they had threatened to shoot them if they broke out. It was reasoned that there was little danger of the Germans carrying out their threat so long as the Norwegians were close by.

"We've got to do this better next time, lads," said one of the officers as they held an "inquest" on their last unsuccessful attempt at attracting the attention of the Norwegians. It was decided that when the Norwegian ship came close again there should be one man stationed in readiness with a whistle at the forward lookout, and another with a Red Ensign tied to a broom stick at the after position.

"Now!" The lookout flung out the word and the officer with the whistle blew the S.O.S. like a man demented, while the Red Ensign was pushed up through the after hatch. This was the signal for the winches to start again and for a fight for the Red Ensign between the Britishers inside the hatch and the Germans outside. The Germans won the uneven struggle, and for good measure let go with their hoses again. Soaked and defeated, the prisoners collapsed exhausted. It was heartbreaking. Were all their struggles to be in vain? "Surely to God, the Norwegians have heard us?" said Cyril Smith.

Did the Norwegians hear them? In the earlier inspections, it could be regarded as doubtful. Now it was a different matter. There was a sense of urgency on the part of the Norwegians. The *Garm* had halted the *Altmark* off Stureholmen in Hjeltefjord, which was seven nautical miles within the northern limit of the Bergen Defended Area. The *Snogg* was then ordered alongside the *Garm*, and her captain instructed to enlarge on the details concerning his inspection of the *Altmark*.

Rear-Admiral Tank-Nielsen listened intently as the facts of the boarding of the *Altmark* were stated. He came to the conclusion that the question as to whether or not the *Altmark* was a warship or a merchant vessel was still in doubt. Did she have any prisoners on board? That was another matter about which there still had not been any satisfactory explanation. The whole situation bristled with uncertainties. This was a cat and mouse game, and so far Dau was winning. Captain Stamso and Commander Simensen, of the *Snogg*, were given orders to go aboard the *Altmark* to make another inspection.

Third Officer Schmidt was on the bridge when he saw the Norwegians approaching and making ready to come aboard. Dau was pacing the bridge wing and muttering to himself. "I know, I know. . . ." He gestured impatiently as Schmidt was about to speak. "We have the Norwegians again!" Dau exclaimed as there was a clatter of seaboots on the deck.

"This is outrageous," he expostulated as the Norwegian officers met him on the bridge. "I'm sorry, Herr Kapitaen, but we are not entirely satisfied about your ship," said Captain Stamso. "We must know more details and make a thorough examination."

Dau was horrified. A thorough search of the storerooms would reveal his human cargo. He must continue to bluff.

"I see no reason why you should not be satisfied, gentlemen," he said. "I have already been inspected and everything was found satisfactory. I cannot afford any more delay. The British will have a greater chance of finding my ship in the Skagerrak if you do not permit me to proceed."

"I am afraid I have no choice in the matter, Herr Kapitaen. My Admiral insists that you provide the information we require," Captain Stamso told Dau, who was becoming increasingly agitated.

Dau still refused to co-operate and once more pointed out that the *Altmark* was a ship in the service of the state. He then went on to say that the *Altmark* carried certain equipment that must remain secret. His superiors had directed that he must not let his ship be searched.

The prisoners could not understand why, with all the noise they were making, the Norwegians gave no sign of being aware that the *Altmark* was carrying prisoners. The *Altmark* also had Norwegian pilots aboard. Someone among the Norwegians must have seen or heard some unusual activity. It was virtually impossible in the circumstances to do otherwise, and this was to be borne out by subsequent Norwegian accounts of this controversial episode in Norway's maritime history. The Norwegians were, however, now playing it by the book, if at the same time, as it was to be alleged, turning a blind eye to certain factors.

Dau was still protesting to the Norwegian officers about being boarded again, and was then told that the ship would have to be searched only if he insisted that he wished to pass through the Bergen

War Harbour. This gave an opening for Dau, who said he would navigate outside the war harbour while still keeping within Norwegian territorial waters.

It was while this was in progress that Dau came to the conclusion that it was time he contacted the German authorities as the matter was reaching serious proportions. He attempted to send a telegram to the German Legation in Oslo, asking them to make a complaint about the *Altmark* being delayed, which he considered was contrary to international law. He said he had already given the Norwegians the information they had requested, but was now being stopped again. Dau, in sending the telegram, had flouted Norwegian regulations forbidding this, and the message was intercepted by the *Garm*.

There was much discussion in official Norwegian circles. The *Westerwald* had caused enough difficulties and now the *Altmark* was a further embarrassment. The first hint that the Norwegians believed there might be prisoners aboard the *Altmark* came in a message from the 2nd Naval Defence District, reported to the Norwegian First Sea Lord, Rear-Admiral H. Diesen. This stated that Dau had refused a further inspection and therefore passage through the defended area was not permitted. Prisoners of war were likely to be aboard.

This led to discussion at high level. Some decision had to be taken, and eventually it was decided that the *Altmark*, being a state ship and not a warship, should be permitted to pass through the defended area.

Accordingly, the *Altmark* was to be allowed to go in her "capacity of a state ship", but with escort. This meant that she could pass through the defended area. It seemed that all was now set fair for the tanker. Dau had earlier been aboard the *Garm* after hailing the Norwegian destroyer and asking her to pass on a message to the German Legation in Oslo. Rear-Admiral Tank-Nielsen had told Dau he must come aboard the *Garm*. The German captain was received aboard the *Garm* correctly, and there was an official German request that the *Altmark* should be allowed through the defended area. This, the Norwegians stated, had already been agreed.

As the *Altmark* prepared to be on her way again, the prisoners were in an agony of suspense. Conditions were foul. They were unable to get out of the flats and any attempt to do so would be met with another deluge of ice-cold water.

Melville-Evans, in what was to be his final entry, was writing in his diary that the sight of Norwegian warships had started them off in another near-riot, but as the hatches had been secured with wire and the lights were turned off again, there seemed little chance of making a real attempt at a breakout. It was agreed that a search party was bound to come aboard, so they calmed down, taking turns at the peephole with whistles at the ready to sound S.O.S.

"But," he wrote, "only two men came on board, stayed amidships for 10 minutes then left. That was the only search." (This was obviously a reference to the visit by the *Garm*.)

The prisoners were also feeling hungry as the only food they had had for two days was hard biscuits, washed down with water. The chats about meals they would like to enjoy if free and the writing of menus on the back of the chart were things of the past. The thought was of freedom rather than meals, though pangs of hunger kept reminding them that they were in need of warm food. They could not wash, the latrine drums had not been emptied for three days, their clothes and the decks were damp from the water the Germans had hosed down on them during the riots, and it seemed that they were to be denied freedom.

The German crew were feeling more optimistic now that they had been allowed to proceed. There was talk of reaching Kiel on the Saturday. Otto Schmidt had passed on this information to the prisoners, and it fitted in with their own assumptions. It now began to look as if the Navy had failed them, and as if the Norwegians did not want to know of their presence or were deliberately ignoring it. "They don't want to be involved," was the opinion of one officer as the officers discussed the situation. There was general agreement on this and a feeling of sadness that the Norwegians should be letting them down in this way. They were turning a blind eye to prisoners being aboard, it was thought.

The prisoners would probably have modified their views had they had a fuller understanding of the situation. The Germans had not hoodwinked the Norwegians as completely as they thought. Men in high positions in Norway were anxious to be rid of this tanker that seemed to have eluded the British Navy ever since leaving the South Atlantic, but Norwegian officers on the spot were seeing things in a different light.

Rear-Admiral Tank-Nielsen thought that it was wrong to let the tanker go and that the instruction to do so was in conflict with the neutrality regulations.

Men in the *Garm* and in the *Snogg* had been observing and hearing some unusual activity and noise from the *Altmark*. One of the

Norwegians who had doubts about the *Altmark* was a young signalman in the *Snogg* by the name of Harald Ronneberg. The *Snogg* was secured alongside the *Garm* and he and his fellow crew members became aware of strange whistling sounds, knockings and other noises. The young signalman, who was doing his national service and was later to gain a commission in the Royal Norwegian Navy and attain the rank of commodore, pondered on the goings-on in this strange ship over which such a fuss seemed to be being made.

If the Norwegian seamen were wondering what was going on in the *Altmark*, then at least one man of higher rank was concerned enough to make a report. The officer was Captain Stamso, who reported that while the *Garm* was in hailing distance, those on board could hear S.O.S. signals from the *Altmark*. There was also the clatter of winches, from which was drawn the conclusion that they were set in motion to cover the sound of the S.O.S. signals. In addition, men could be seen waving from portholes, which were suddenly closed. It was felt that there were prisoners on board.

With the all-clear from the Norwegians, Dau thought that, despite the delay, the *Altmark* was in a position to reach Kiel safely, if only she could avoid the British patrols. For the moment at least, things seemed to be going their way, he thought. They had had a lot of luck, he acknowledged to himself, and with a little more they might yet outwit the accursed British.

Signals were flashing from the *Snogg*. It was time to be under way. Dau rang down to the engine room and slowly, with the *Snogg* as escort, *Altmark* moved off to pass through the defended area. The *Snogg* escorted the *Altmark* from Bjornsund Lighthouse until relieved by her sister ship *Stegg* in Bjornefjord, south of Bergen. At noon on that day, 16th February, the patrol boat *Firern* took over as escort at Jaeren Rev, south of Stavanger.

There was a feeling of despair in the prisoners' flats in the *Altmark*. Escorted by the Norwegians, the *Altmark* was edging her way home and it seemed that little could now stop her. The conditions in the flats were growing worse, and the stench from the latrine drums was nauseating. The men were making what meal they could from the hard biscuits that had been issued now that they were confined below decks. The water with which they had to make do in place of hot tea tasted brackish.

Some of the prisoners were beginning to submit to a feeling of hopelessness. They were like men who had attacked their cell wall only to find after breaking through one wall that another confronted them, and still another. They had tried and tried to let the Norwegians know they were in the *Altmark*, but nothing they did, it seemed, could bring them the freedom for which they yearned. The Norwegians did not care, apparently, and the Royal Navy must have ceased to hunt for the *Altmark*. There was nothing for it but Germany and a prison camp.

The men sat around in groups talking and generally agreeing their chances of rescue were becoming slimmer by the hour. There was now little contact with the Germans, apart from the guards. Dr Tyrolt was doing his best to ease their suffering and had had an extractor fan fitted in the prison quarters in an effort to clear the air of the stench from the latrine drums. He had also arranged for air to be forced through the flats under pressure to make conditions easier.

The men's clothing was now filthy, and the decks were grubby. There was little room in which to move due to the suitcases packed ready and waiting for the rescue that now seemed as far away as ever.

Apart from the doctor, anxious to protect the health of the prisoners so far as was possible in the conditions, the Germans generally had enough to do trying to bluff the Norwegians and endeavouring to get the *Altmark* through these dangerous waters, without concerning themselves over the captives. If the British saw their chance of escape fading away, so the German crew, for their part, feared that they would fail to reach home by some ill-fortune in the last hours of their voyage. The pressure they were under was such that they had little time to think of the prisoners. They were just as anxious as Dau that the *Altmark* be allowed to proceed without being searched.

First Officer Paulsen and Third Officer Schmidt paced the bridge and watched the Norwegian escort. "At least they are letting us continue," said Paulsen. "I thought when the destroyer arrived that she would send a boarding party and insist on searching us. We could not have stopped them."

Schmidt agreed. "I do not think the Norwegians really knew what to do with us when we arrived," he commented, watching the patrol boat through the bridge windows. "I am of the opinion that there has been much talk in Oslo and Bergen about what to do with us. The defended area they speak of makes it difficult for them to give us passage. But now we seem to be on our way without difficulty. I hope it is so."

"If we can avoid the British Navy for just a few more hours, I think we will be safely home," Paulsen stated as he swept the sea with his glasses. "If we are caught by the British, then it will be us who will spend the war in a prison camp." He shuddered at the thought.

Despite their despondency, the prisoners were still maintaining an alert lookout. They had been aware of the *Firern* taking over escort duty, but apart from that nothing of note had occurred for some time.

Suddenly, the lookout shouted from his perch, "Quiet! I can hear engines. They sound like aircraft. Yes! Yes! They're coming in low. The Germans have their belongings on deck, making for the boats. It's the R.A.F., lads. The blooming R.A.F.!"

9

The Hunters

Ever since the scuttling of the *Graf Spee*, the Royal Navy hunting groups had been trying to comply with the First Lord of the Admiralty's "scrub and search" order for the *Altmark*. Every effort was being made to locate this tanker that seemed to have disappeared with the prisoners that the Merchant Navy officers released from the *Graf Spee* had reported were on board. Messages from the British Naval Attachés in Montevideo and Buenos Aires kept the Admiralty informed of developments in the South Atlantic.

The Naval Attaché in Montevideo was reporting after the Battle of the River Plate and the release of the captives from the *Graf Spee* that he had learned from the captain of the *Doric Star*, Captain Stubbs, that the *Tairoa* had been sunk by the pocket battleship on 3rd December and that the raider had oiled from the *Altmark* on 6th December, sinking the *Streonshalh* the following day. The *Altmark* was described as being painted black, with a white deckhouse, a yellow funnel with NORGE painted on the bridge deckhouse, and flying the Norwegian flag. It was understood that she was prepared to use the letters U.S.S.R. and to fly that flag. The Attaché added that he had also been informed that she had concealed guns behind the deckhouse.

The picture was beginning to build up. The British Naval Attaché in Buenos Aires also sent a report giving information from released captives from the *Graf Spee* who had been prisoners in the supply ship. It was learned from these accounts that the *Altmark* had taken on board fuel oil in Texas during August, and had last topped up the *Graf Spee* on 6th December in approximate position 023° South 026° West. It was normal for her to cruise between the positions 10° and 20° South and 10° and 20° West. This area was described as a "super doldrum", making it easy for small boats to move between the *Altmark* and the *Graf Spee* with supplies and men without any problems. The *Altmark* had once remained there for four days, and was believed to have left the area only during the time when the pocket battleship was marauding in the Indian Ocean. It was thought that the tanker went south and east of the Cape.

The possibility of something going wrong had also been gone into, and in the event of the *Altmark* and the *Graf Spee* failing to meet after a certain time limit had expired, the tanker was under orders to make for either Bahia or Pernambuco. The tanker was a vessel of about 20,000 tons and was said to be able to carry a cargo of 14,000 tons of oil. It was also said that she had a top speed of more than 25 knots. The reports from the former prisoners revealed she had ammunition magazines, large storerooms, refrigeration, sixteen derricks and two large guns hidden behind flaps on which NORGE was painted. Two 3-centimetre pom-poms were fixed on the bridge.

It was obvious that those held captive in the *Altmark* had been observing everything, judging from the details they gave on release from the *Graf Spee*. They reported that the method of oiling was to tow the ship being oiled astern. The oil line was supported by stirrups from the towing hawser. Cork floats were wrapped around the pipe at frequent intervals.

Questions were put to the former prisoners about the possibility of the *Altmark* having provided fuel for U-boats. They said that the *Altmark* had not oiled any U-boat, nor had they heard any mention in the *Altmark* or the *Graf Spee* of any U-boat being in the area.

The character of the *Altmark* master, Dau, also came in for consideration. He was described as a reserve officer of the old school and bore a grudge against the British, having been a prisoner in the First World War. "He was a stern disciplinarian, feared, respected and disliked." The *Altmark* crew were made to sound a rough lot, being termed hard-bitten and discontented. They did not get on with the guards placed on board the *Altmark* from the *Graf Spee*, and the bitterness was such that at times fights broke out between them. Conditions for the prisoners were harsh, and could be compared with those in the days of the slave-traders.

It was a grim picture the captives were painting, and one that was at variance with subsequent accounts from prisoners released from the *Altmark* in Jossingfjord. The Indians, it was claimed, were treated much better than the white prisoners. The motive was political, it was said. Conditions in the flats came in for strong criticism. There were stories of mattresses almost walking on their own with the lice and vermin that bred in them. Water was in short supply as was soap. The captives had to share twenty bowls between them for washing purposes.

Men who had roughed it in many ports of the world and served in ships of all kinds were loud in their complaints of the catering arrangements in the *Altmark*. Condensed milk tins were used as eating utensils and the bottoms of big tins were cut out to serve as plates. Food was short and what there was of it was of poor quality.

Dau had often spoken of burning his ship if discovered, but the released British Merchant Navy officers stated that Dau had said that he would blow her up with the prisoners on board if any British warship came upon the *Altmark*.

The reports of those released from the *Graf Spee* were filling in the outlines of the vessel that had been the handmaiden of the pocket battleship and was now herself being sought by the hunting groups freed of their quest for the raider. One man in a good position to report on both the *Altmark* and the *Graf Spee* was Chief Officer A. H. Thompson, of the *Huntsman*. He was the officer whose organizing ability had impressed the Germans when the *Huntsman* crew had been taken aboard the *Altmark*, and was one of those transferred back to the *Graf Spee*.

The transfer took place on 28th November, when all captains, chief officers, second officers, chief engineers, second engineers and radio officers were told to pack a suitcase or parcel of clothes, and to change their beds for hammock beds with some of those who had been provided with hammock beds from the *Graf Spee*. A total of twenty-seven men, including two assistant stewards, was sent across to the *Graf Spee* by motor launch.

They were able to greet the crews of the *Doric Star* and the *Tairoa* when these men arrived on board after capture by the raider. Fifty-one men were now packed into a small room, and on the last meeting with the *Altmark* on 6th December the second officers, second engineers and the two stewards who had been transferred from the tanker were sent back, along with the crews of the *Doric Star* and the *Tairoa*. Captain Brown, master of the *Huntsman*, and Captain Starr, of the *Tairoa*, also went to the *Altmark*.

Captain Pottinger, of the *Ashlea*, in commenting about the *Graf Spee*, thought that Langsdorff was a fine man and not a coward. The crew, he believed, had just gone to pieces after the Battle of the River Plate. Many were aged between seventeen and twenty-two, and there was no fight left in them after the battle. Rather surprisingly, he made the point that discipline was slack, and that the men were allowed to "lounge" and took little notice of the officers. They were far from smart, which was not in accord with the Germans' known reputation for smartness and discipline.

Captain Dove, master of the *Africa Shell*, sunk when the *Graf Spee* had slipped into the Indian Ocean for a time in order to confuse the hunting groups, reported on the meeting with the *Altmark* on 26th November. The Germans had a party on board that evening and invited him to attend. Captain Dove refused the invitation, but this did not prevent the Germans from going to his cabin and toasting his health, saying he would be a prisoner the following day. He was bombarded with questions when the other British officers were ferried across to the *Graf Spee* on 28th November. They had not believed it when told he was aboard.

Captain Dove was surprised when Langsdorff committed suicide and considered him "a very humane man". He was "a gentleman and much too humane for the job he was doing. He should never have taken it on". Langsdorff had told him that he was not going to put to sea with 1,100 men with the *Graf Spee* as she was. It would be suicide to do so. "I have only beggar boys for crew, very few sailors," he had said.

While other captains and officers confessed to a grudging admiration for Langsdorff, Captain Edwards, master of the *Trevanion*, was in no doubt over his views of the German commander. He was convinced that Langsdorff was a liar and was too confident; everything he said turned out to be untrue. He kept a bad lookout at sea, and as for the crew, they had the mentality of children. Many had come direct from farms and had never before seen the sea. They were "scared stiff" while the *Graf Spee* was hove to during the sinking of the *Tairoa*, anticipating a British warship to be seen approaching over the horizon at any moment. They were good at sinking merchant ships that could not defend themselves, but it was a different story when it came to a fight with the British cruisers.

Captain Edwards was also outspoken about his experiences in the *Altmark*. They were treated badly and Lieutenant Schmidt, in charge of the guard, behaved terribly towards the prisoners. The food was also bad.

The master of the *Streonshalh*, Captain Robinson, was also impressed by the age of the crew, which he put at between nineteen and twenty-two. He, too, was of the opinion that they lacked discipline.

The reports of the captains to the British authorities seemed to point to the fact that the *Graf Spee* had not been so efficiently manned as thought, and that the *Altmark* was a ship at war within herself, with the crew and the *Graf Spee* guards at loggerheads and the master feared by all.

But where was the elusive *Altmark*? The hunt went on, and then, five days before Christmas 1939, there came a glimmer of hope. A message went out from the Admiralty to the C-in-C, South Atlantic, stating that there was a chance of intercepting the tanker if Force K, *Neptune* and *Severn*, swept to the south-east for forty-eight hours and then swept towards Freetown. The signal ended "Comply". *Neptune* and *Severn* were only too anxious to comply, but they did not sight the *Altmark*.

The year dragged to a close with no sighting of the *Altmark* despite intense efforts to prevent the tanker slipping through the net. Could things be better in the New Year? It seemed so. On 1st January 1940 there was hardly time to exchange the customary "Happy New Year" greetings when a flurry of signals pushed the New Year celebrations out of mind. A report was received of an unidentified tanker.

H.M.S. *Effingham* and H.M.S. *Ascania* were alerted. They received a signal from the C-in-C America and West Indies. It read: "Unknown tanker answers description *Altmark* was in position 022° 54′ North 053° 36′ West at 1600Z 28th Dec., proceeding in north-easterly direction at high speed. This ship may possibly cross your track within the next 48 hours."

A keen watch was kept, but still the *Altmark* remained free. It was during this period that she was lurking in the South Atlantic undergoing an overhaul of her engines and generally preparing for her breakout later in January. So long as she stayed in the South Atlantic, the *Altmark* stood a good chance of remaining undetected. She had done so while supplying the *Graf Spee*, and, in her turn, the pocket battleship had remained elusive despite the hunting groups that had been searching for her. The *Graf Spee* might have eluded the hunting groups for a great deal longer had not Langsdorff made the fatal error of mistaking the British cruisers for a convoy screen. Had he been aware of his mistake in time, he could have taken the *Graf Spee* out of imminent danger until another defenceless merchantman fell into his net. He might well in the end have completed his mission and made the dash back to Germany.

Whereas the *Graf Spee* would have been a match for most of the British warships she might have encountered and have stood a fair chance of getting away with it unless confronted with overwhelming odds, the *Altmark* was in no position to try conclusions with a warship.

Her one hope lay in her speed and ability to remain hidden and to see before being seen. She had a crew of experienced seamen and an even more experienced captain. The captains and officers released at Montevideo had given a comprehensive account of the tanker and the conditions in her. It was apparent, then, that the *Altmark* would wish to make an attempt to reach Germany as soon as possible.

The Admiralty could, however, only guess where she was likely to be. They could not be aware of the decision to hide in the South Atlantic and to repair the engines. The only thing of which they could be certain was that sooner or later Dau was going to have to risk detection. That risk was likely to be greater when he was on the last leg of the voyage. The Norwegian coast was a place that offered a good chance of the tanker being spotted. It would not be long then before reports reached London of her presence. The question would then arise as to how to deal with the *Altmark* if she remained within Norwegian territorial waters.

The whole situation bristled with problems. Once through territorial waters and in the Skagerrak the problem of intercepting the *Altmark* would be greater. There was also the question of correct identification of the *Altmark* in those waters with so much other shipping in the area. Naval units would be spread out and could waste time intercepting vessels that, while bearing some resemblance to the *Altmark*, were not her. The *Altmark* was also reported to have adopted different disguises.

Aircraft, too, would be faced with difficulty if conditions were not good, and would probably have to swoop down to deck level to make a positive identification. It was not a matter of turning up an identification book as in the case of a warship, and saying that she was such and such a class or even ship. The *Altmark* was a tanker purely and simply, if her armament was ignored, and could be one of a dozen others that had lawful passage along the coast.

No; the hunters would really have to do the hunting to single out their quarry from a busy field. There were likely to be a few false hares raised before the right one was found and run to earth. This was to be proved true. In the meantime, preparations were made to snare the *Altmark* as she made her last desperate bid for home.

The moves about to be set in motion to corner the *Altmark* once and for all were to lead to some of the most exciting action of the war, even if it was to be on a small scale compared with battleships and cruisers exchanging shells at long distance with individual victims cut down by knife-edged splinters, just nameless foes to their opponents. This was to be an affair of man-to-man with a dash of the old man-o'-war tactics about it. There were to be shots and screams and death in the icy water before the affair was ended.

The stage was being set at the windswept Royal Naval base at Rosyth, in the Firth of Forth, and on a bleak airfield in North Yorkshire.

10

Altmark Your Objective

It was St Valentine's Day, 14th February, when Operation D.T. got under way. Late that evening five destroyers and two cruisers left Rosyth. They were the destroyers *Cossack* (Captain [D] 4th Destroyer Flotilla Senior Officer), *Sikh*, *Nubian*, *Intrepid*, *Ivanhoe* and the cruisers *Arethusa* and *Penelope*. The reason ostensibly was an ice reconnaissance. The real reason could not be hidden, however, for all destroyers had embarked boarding parties before sailing. The *Arethusa* had provided four of these, and the men in the parties knew that there was something more important afoot than checking on the ice situation.

Captain Philip Vian was flotilla leader, Captain (D). The striking force was *Cossack*, *Sikh*, *Nubian*, forming the first division; *Ivanhoe* and *Intrepid*, the second division, and *Penelope* and *Arethusa*, the third division. The flotilla received an early setback, however, when *Penelope* fouled a baffle and had to drop out of the operation.

Lookouts were constantly alert for mines as well as other vessels and early on the morning of 15th February, German floating mines were seen bobbing dangerously in the water and were sunk.

There was a moment of drama when lookouts reported lights. The *Intrepid* was ordered to investigate the mysterious vessel. She was a trawler carrying fishing lights and showing Dutch colours. The *Mindjerk*, for such she turned out to be, had fishing gear over the side. Commander R. C. Gordon, satisfied that the vessel was harmless, gave the order for his ship to join the rest of the flotilla.

The force sailed on without further incident until at 2230 hours Commander Gordon found *Intrepid* called upon to undertake another spot of investigating. Two tankers had earlier been reported to be anchored in Listerfjord.

Intrepid altered course and Commander Gordon and the other officers swept the sea with their glasses as the destroyer surged ahead to the limit of Norwegian territorial waters as close as possible to the position reported.

"Well, they don't seem to be there," said the commander. "They could have gone into one of the fjords." He ordered a patrol to seaward during the night, but nothing was sighted and at daylight rejoined the striking force.

The operation, so far as the ice reconnaissance was concerned, was showing results. The *Arethusa* ran into pancake ice, which gradually thickened. The ice was so thick on one occasion that the port paravane backhaul was torn away with the sheer weight of the ice.

Messages were coming in from the Admiralty, and one of these gave the position in which the *Altmark* had been sighted at 1600 hours on 14th February, in the afternoon of the day on which the force had sailed from Rosyth. A further message reported that the tanker had passed Bergen at noon that day, 15th February. This news led Captain (D) to decide to recast the sweep completely in order to nobble the ship that had cocked a snook at the Royal Navy for so long. The search was transferred from a position to the south of Kristiansand to a position near the Little Fisher Bank.

Then, with 16th February only forty-eight minutes old, Captain Vian received "a most immediate" message from the Commander-in-Chief, Home Fleet, Sir Charles Forbes. This ordered Captain (D) to make *Altmark* the chief objective of the operation. There was now no doubt—the *Altmark* was to be hunted down. The Navy that the prisoners in the *Altmark* had prayed for, cursed and hoped for during their long months in captivity was now sweeping towards them determined on rescue. The force was spread on a line six miles apart and swept northward along the route used by German ships from Utsire to pass eastward of the German minefield. The force was also assisted by submarines, H.M.S. *Seal* reporting that the quarry had not yet passed southward of Skudesnesfjord.

But the operation was not confined to the Navy, even though it was really their "show", anxious as they were to snare the *Altmark*. The Royal Air Force had a hand in things. Hudsons from Thornaby-on-Tees were flying patrols and keeping a sharp lookout for the tanker that was likely to be hugging the coast and merging into the background. It was also not easy to pick out the right tanker from others of a similar type in those waters, with ice, fog and flurries of snow all contributing to make sighting difficult.

A battle flight of three Hudsons took off from Thornaby on the morning of 15th February to carry out an "unostentatious reconnaissance" into the Skagerrak to report on ice conditions near the coast and movements of any merchant ships they might sight.

Flying Officer Tullock and Sergeant Knowles in one Hudson, Flying Officer Fleetwood and Pilot Officer Lawrie in the second, with Flying Officer Wright and Pilot Officer Mitchell in the third, swept the sea for any signs of merchant ships. Snow showers did not help matters. They saw a few merchant vessels and reported that the Norwegian and Danish coasts in that locality seemed to be free from ice. There was some consolation in the fact that the weather over there was fine and clear, and the crews were even able to admire the snow-covered coastline.

The Hudsons landed at 1535 hours after being airborne six hours and 35 minutes. Earlier that day another flight had reported that one cruiser and five destroyers—the striking force—had left the Firth of Forth on an easterly course. By eight o'clock that morning—the 15th—the force from Rosyth was reported to have reached a position opposite Dyce, going north-east.

Thornaby was playing a vital part in the hunt for the *Altmark*, and the talk on the station as the crews were briefed or chatted over mugs of "char" was of this ship that was the subject of a flap. The tension built up when, at 1810 hours on the 15th, a message was received at Thornaby saying that it had been reported from Bergen that the *Altmark*, with British prisoners on board, would pass Bergen at noon, but the date could not be ascertained.

It was later confirmed that the *Altmark* had passed Bergen at noon on the 15th. The description given was that of a tanker of 20,000 tons with black hull, white deckhouse, yellow funnel, with NORGE painted on the bridge deckhouse, and flying the Norwegian flag. She was said to be armed with three 6-inch guns and also anti-aircraft guns of unknown size. (This, of course, did not fit in with the reports of *Altmark* using her original name on entering Norwegian territorial waters and of flying the German state flag, over which there was so much controversy. The vessel was reported to have about 400 prisoners on board, which again was guesswork. But the aircraft crew who sighted her were apparently in no doubt about the flag.)

The cruiser and five destroyers were, at 0001 hours on 16th February, reported to be just off the south coast of Norway at the Skagerrak. The striking force was being "shadowed" in that two Hudsons had taken off before dawn with orders to cross the North Sea to the vicinity of the Danish coast and then separate, flying on different tracks to the South Norwegian coast. Their orders were to try to locate the British striking force, but there was also another reason for the mission. The Hudsons were also to try to pinpoint the *Altmark*.

This was what was needed, the actual position of the *Altmark*. The tanker seemed to be thwarting all efforts to pin her down. Ships were investigating every craft in sight and aircraft were swooping out of the sky at the least sight of anything that could possibly be the *Altmark*. Hudson A/220 landed at 1045 hours, but the crew had nothing to report except floating ice to a depth of 30 miles off the Danish coast.

Twenty minutes later, L/220 landed, and had had some luck in that they had spotted a German motor vessel, the *Hermod*, of 2,500 tons. Of the *Altmark*, there was not a sign. She seemed to have just merged into the Norwegian coastline, seemingly a ghost ship in that she appeared and vanished at will. The crews of the Hudsons reported for de-briefing and a welcome rest after being in the air since 0510 hours.

The R.A.F. was not to be put off by this setback. Three more Hudsons had in the meantime taken off. Hudsons K, M and V took off at 0825 hours on a similar flight. Their orders were to locate and report any merchant ship of more than 10,000 tons. They were also to keep an eye open for the striking force of the cruiser and destroyers in this region.

The air became alive with news of sightings of the *Altmark*. It was 1224 when Thornaby received a message that the tanker had been spotted at noon close to the south-west coast of Norway. A later signal gave the *Altmark*'s position as two miles off the Norwegian coast with her speed estimated at six knots. Other messages intercepted between the three Hudsons and group gave more news of the *Altmark*'s progress. But was she really the *Altmark*? The sighting reports seemed to be coming thick and fast.

There was nothing to do but wait. Sooner or later there was bound to be definite identification of the *Altmark*. Once her identity was established it was a job for the Navy. The R.A.F. could not attack her because of the risk to the prisoners on board, notwithstanding the fact that she was also probably sailing well within Norwegian territorial waters.

The signal they were waiting for came at 1255 hours. Hudson K/220, with Pilot Officer McNeill at the controls, swooped down to investigate the ship the crew of the Hudson had sighted. There was no doubt about it, she was the *Altmark*. Her name could be seen quite clearly. The "enemy first sighting" report was sent out. The three Hudsons, their mission completed, turned for home and landed at

Thornaby at 1620 hours, eighty minutes after their E.T.A. (estimated time of arrival). The crews had been flying over the sea for almost eight hours, but before they enjoyed a welcome meal and a rest they were able to give an up-to-the-minute description of the *Altmark*.

The moment the Hudson swooped out of the sky and sent the crew of the *Altmark* scurrying from one side of the deck to the other, was also the time that Dau realized that he could bluff no more. The British had finally found him for certain and their warships would soon be on to him. The roar of the aircraft overhead and the shout from the British lookout in the tanker that it was the R.A.F., was also the moment that the captives realized that they now had a good chance of being rescued after their months of captivity.

The arrival of the British aircraft had been so sudden that there was no time for them to be properly identified by the *Altmark*. Third Officer Schmidt was of the opinion that they were Blenheims. They rounded the ship and one—apparently the Hudson flown by Pilot Officer McNeill—crossed the tanker at a low height.

Meanwhile, Captain Vian was having problems over the identity of the *Altmark*. Since the "*Altmark* your objective" message, every effort had been made to track down the supply ship, but it was becoming obvious from the sighting reports that several different vessels were being reported as the *Altmark*.

There was also the added difficulty that the hunters were not really sure what the tanker looked like. Then came a bit of luck in the form of a copy of the *Illustrated London News* containing an illustration of two vessels, one reported to be the *Altmark*. One of the vessels was a four-masted ship and the other looked like a tanker, but which one was the *Altmark* was not made clear. Captain (D) and his officers were of the opinion that it was the four-masted vessel, which did not help matters. The Hudson's "enemy first sighting" report clarified matters somewhat, but still no surface vessel had sighted the *Altmark*.

There was another incident early on the morning of the 16th when a vessel was sighted. She was boarded and found to be Dutch, the *Libia*, showing Dutch colours and markings. It was at this point that an officer who was to make his mark in the operation that lay ahead made use of his knowledge of the German and Dutch languages. He was Paymaster Sub-Lieutenant Geoffrey Craven, R.N.V.R., serving in the *Cossack*, who questioned the crew of the trawler and satisfied himself that they really were Dutch.

Early afternoon brought an event that caused some red faces and not a few curses. An aircraft was spotted and was mistaken for a German reconnaissance aircraft. The ships blazed away, but the plane was a Hudson that had fired the wrong grenade challenge. Signal lamp shutters clacked, but the cheeky Hudson refused to reply for some reason best known to themselves. They were lucky not to be blown out of the sky by men whose nerves were already at full stretch after hours of scanning the sea for the *Altmark*.

Sighting reports kept being received, but there was a difference in location of up to twenty-five miles. The force was divided and swept north to Egero and south to Lister. There was plenty of shipping, but where was the *Altmark*?

The long quest took a decisive turn at 1350 hours, Friday, 16th February, when, as *Arethusa* was making her sweep, the gunnery officer, Lieutenant G. O. Roberts, reported from the director control tower: "Ship bearing 020°". She was close to the Norwegian coast and, he reported, closely resembled the *Altmark*. He had the advantage over the bridge as the officers there could not make out the tanker due to the fact that she merged so well into the background of rocks and snow. Captain Q. D. Graham immediately signalled Captain (D) with this bearing.

The gunnery officer was certain that this vessel was the one they sought, and there was no doubt when this was confirmed by the masthead lookout. Captain Graham again alerted Captain Vian in the *Cossack*. It was still not possible to make out the *Altmark* from the bridge of the cruiser. The tanker was at this time some eight or ten miles distant.

Captain Vian wasted no time. The cruiser swung northwards as Vian ordered her to investigate this latest sighting, which was the most concrete they had received apart from the "enemy first sighting" report from the Hudson. If the gunnery officer was right—and it seemed that he was—then there should soon be an end to the affair.

The *Arethusa*'s gun crews were closed up and the guns trained on the ship, which was going along slowly about one mile offshore and inside territorial waters. Now there was no doubt that she was the ship they had been seeking for so long. "It's the *Altmark* all right," said Captain Graham as he trained his glasses on the tanker. She was now plain to see from the bridge. The German flag and the name *Altmark* could be seen.

But what was this? She was being escorted by a torpedo-boat. A German? No; she was Norwegian. The *Arethusa* captain took stock of the situation, and ordered a signal to be made to the *Altmark*. The signal shutter clacked ordering the tanker to steam westward. Flag signals were also made, but the *Altmark* sailed on through a fleet of fishing boats without acknowledging the signals.

The destroyers *Intrepid* and *Ivanhoe* were now on the scene. Captain Graham turned to the signalman: "Make to *Intrepid*, 'Go in and board *Altmark*. I will cover you.'" *Intrepid* was to bring her out of territorial waters if possible. *Intrepid* swung in towards the land and closed *Altmark* with *Ivanhoe* in company. Dau ignored signals hoisted by the destroyers to "Stop your vessel instantly" and to "Steer to westward." Dau had no intention of complying with the orders and continued to hug the coast and steer towards Jossingfjord, with the torpedo-boat to seaward of her and a Norwegian seaplane also in attendance.

Patience was running out and Captain Graham ordered "Make to *Intrepid* 'Capture ship at all costs.'" Another signal a few minutes later read: "Capture the ship." It was apparent that the *Altmark* had no intention of surrendering, and *Ivanhoe* went inshore of the tanker in an effort to drive her out to sea, while Commander Gordon, of the *Intrepid*, ordered a salvo to be fired with the same object in view.

"She's stopped," someone in *Intrepid* said. This appeared to be true. "Lower the whaler." Bluejackets in *Intrepid* hastened to carry out the order. The boarding party, already prepared, pushed off from the destroyer. The Norwegian torpedo-boat was not helping matters, and, in fact, seemed to be trying her best to impede the operation. The Norwegian even came alongside and made a protest.

While all this was in progress, the whaler was nearing the *Altmark*, which suddenly went ahead again. She was now close to the entrance to Jossingfjord, with *Ivanhoe* astern of her.

Commander Gordon, seeing their quarry slipping away, instructed *Ivanhoe* to follow the tanker into the fjord and to machine-gun her bridge if she still would not stop. The whaler was recalled.

Altmark, with *Ivanhoe* in pursuit, was about three cables off the entrance to Jossingfjord and steaming at around six knots. If she were to be stopped, then some swift action was called for. *Ivanhoe* began a daring manoeuvre. The destroyer went alongside the *Altmark*'s starboard side, the boarding party standing by. The vital moment came, but just as the boarding party was about to go, the tanker put on speed and swung to port. The destroyer had to sheer off. The *Ivanhoe* was not to be put off, but by the time she was ideally placed for a second attempt at boarding, the tanker had gone into the inner fjord and two

Norwegian torpedo-boats were making it plain that *Ivanhoe* was not welcome.

This was the position when the *Cossack* arrived and entered Jossingfjord.

For Dau, it was a relief to have entered the fjord and gained some sort of a respite. The *Altmark* had crunched through the ice. With the Norwegian torpedo-boats *Skarv* and *Kjell* in attendance, Dau and his crew felt secure. The pilots left and were handed a cable for the German Legation in Oslo. A Norwegian Customs officer came on board.

Battened down below, the prisoners wondered what was happening. They heard the crunch of ice against the ship's sides as the *Altmark* fled into the fjord. The prisoners guessed by the sound of the ice that they were in a dead end, and that the *Altmark*, if she were to get out, must go by the same way as she had entered. A watch was kept, but they could see very little. They kept quiet compared with the noise they had made on the other occasions, and just before 11 p.m. heard the Germans put their steam jets over the side in an effort to free the *Altmark* from the ice.

The Germans were further relieved when the patrol boat *Firern* entered the fjord after sunset and went alongside a small jetty. The *Skarv*, commanded by Lieutenant H. M. Hansen, had earlier relieved *Firern* of her escort duties. *Firern* had returned to Egersund, but shortly after arriving was ordered to sail for Jossingfjord, where she tied up at the quay at 2040 hours. The torpedo-boat *Kjell*, commanded by Lieutenant F. G. Halvorsen, had arrived a short while after the *Skarv* and in time to prevent *Ivanhoe* following the *Altmark*.

It seemed to be stalemate. Captain Vian, in *Cossack*, at first took the diplomatic action of trying to talk things over with the Norwegians.

This brought no results. Captain Vian sent off a message to the Admiralty at 1616 hours saying that he was in Jossingfjord with the *Altmark* and a Norwegian gunboat. "I have demanded English prisoners," he reported.

Dau was also busy sending signals, calling the Norwegian station Farsund, but the *Arethusa* began jamming and continued doing so until ordered to cease later by Captain (D). One message intercepted by British sources was addressed to the German Legation in Oslo and stated that Dau had been driven inshore by British destroyers. The *Altmark* was now drifting in Jossingfjord, the message added.

The drama of the situation was summed up by Vian in a signal to the

Admiralty, repeated to C-in-C Home Fleet. The message, sent at 1632 hours, read: "Fjord is dead end. I do not expect any change from Norwegian gunboat, who is examining *Altmark*. A second gunboat has a torpedo tube trained on me. *Altmark* is apparently being effectively jammed by H.M.S. *Arethusa*. She is painted warship grey."

Captain Vian had received the report of the captain of the *Ivanhoe*, Commander P. H. Hadow, and also had a confrontation with the commanding officer of the *Kjell*. The Norwegian was not pleased with this intrusion into Norwegian waters, and told Captain Vian so.

The commanding officer of the *Kjell*, Lieutenant Halvorsen, came aboard the *Cossack* at Captain Vian's invitation. Captain (D) did not mince words. He told the Norwegian officer that British prisoners were held in the *Altmark*'s holds and that it was no use maintaining otherwise. Captain Vian wanted the right to see for himself, and wished the Norwegian to accompany him. Lieutenant Halvorsen was having none of this from the British destroyer captain, and pointed out that the Norwegian pilots on board the *Altmark* said the tanker had been examined in Bergen the previous day, 15th February. The vessel was unarmed, and there were no indications of British prisoners being aboard.

It seemed he was prepared to back up his words with force, for the Norwegians had their torpedo tubes trained on the *Cossack*, whose crew were looking on the scene with interest and wondering who was going to come out the best in this contest between their captain and the Norwegian.

What to do next? Captain Vian decided it would be prudent to withdraw from the fjord for the time being, but not before he had received an undertaking from the Norwegian that he would search the *Altmark* while the *Cossack* waited outside. Captain Vian had not much faith that a search would be carried out once the Norwegians saw that the *Cossack* had left the fjord.

Matters were becoming serious. The *Altmark* was in the fjord and the British ships were inside territorial waters, with the Norwegians in the middle of it all. It seemed to them that the foes were simply going to settle their differences in someone else's backyard—in this case the Norwegians'. From a diplomatic point of view, the situation was a delicate one. You do not go and fight your battles on neutral territory. The British could argue that the *Altmark* should not have tried to slip home through territorial waters in the first place. The Norwegians could equally argue that the British had no right to come barnstorming into territorial waters in order to capture an enemy ship, and not a warship at that. But the whole question, in the end, hinged on whether or not the *Altmark* carried British prisoners.

The British felt they had every reason to believe that the tanker did, in fact, carry several hundred of their fellow countrymen and that those same prisoners would be in Germany within a very short time once the *Altmark* left Norwegian waters. It was no time to play the gentleman. If the *Altmark* wanted things the hard way, then so be it.

The situation now called for a decision that Captain Vian could not make on his own. He had tried by all reasonable means to get aboard the *Altmark*, trying to enlist the aid of the Norwegians to clear up the matter of the prisoners. That help had not been forthcoming, and now a higher authority must make the decision on what the next stage of the action was to be.

In London, the Admiralty was fully alerted. Vian's signal concerning the reception from the Norwegian torpedo-boat's commander needed instant action. The scene in the Admiralty War Room was brisk as the orders flowed in. Winston Churchill, as First Lord, now had a chance of settling accounts with the *Altmark*, which had so successfully eluded the hunting units in their "scrub and search" tactics until being sighted off Norway. Churchill wasted no time, and, after obtaining the agreement of the Foreign Secretary, had the following signal sent:

> Unless Norwegian torpedo-boat undertakes to convoy *Altmark* to Bergen with a joint Anglo-Norwegian guard on board, and a joint escort, you should board *Altmark*, liberate the prisoners, and take possession of the ship pending further instructions. If Norwegian torpedo-boat interferes, you should warn her to stand off. If she fires upon you, you should not reply unless attack is serious, in which case you should defend yourself, using no more force than is necessary, and ceasing fire when she desists.

Captain Vian was now in no doubt as to what action he had to take. He ordered the *Cossack* to be taken back into the fjord, where he hoped to reason with the commanding officer of the *Kjell*. The Norwegian officer remained unco-operative. He had, he repeated, no choice in the matter. He was under orders.

The Norwegian found Captain Vian just as obstinate as himself. He suggested that the Norwegian officer should embark the *Cossack*'s party and join them in a search of the *Altmark*. The officer refused this invitation because of the ice conditions. The argument went on, and all the time Captain Vian was becoming more anxious because of the time factor. Once daylight came, there was the possibility that German aircraft would join the fray. Eventually, the officer, Lieutenant Halvorsen, agreed to join the *Cossack* and accompany the boarding officers.

Meanwhile, the Admiralty had been active in sending support for the operation. Three submarines were ordered to be concentrated off Jossingfjord. These were H.M.S. *Seal*, H.M.S. *Triad* and the Polish submarine *Orzel*.

The boarding party was making ready in *Cossack*. About forty-five officers and ratings formed the party, and were organized in four sections. Every man knew his job. Lieutenant-Commander Bradwell Talbot Turner, second-in-command of the *Cossack*, with his party, was to take over the bridge and question the captain. The party under the command of Lieutenant Parker was to secure the bridge structure, while the third party, under the leadership of Gunner James Smith, was to secure the after part, with the last section, led by Petty Officer Norman Atkins, the fore part.

Nerves were taut as the last minutes ticked away before the curtain rose on the last act of the drama.

11

Well done, *Cossack*

Customs' officer Egaas was walking along the road by Jossingfjord when he saw the *Altmark* in the fjord, in which he noticed there was a lot of ice. He had no undue cause for concern. His colleague Giertsen was on board. It had been decided that a full Customs' inspection was not necessary, and that only a Customs' officer should be placed on board to keep watch. The two Norwegian pilots had already gone ashore. Giertsen agreed with Dau that only an ordinary watch should be kept.

Giertsen was on board until 8 p.m. Egaas, who had also gone aboard, went below decks and enjoyed a cup of coffee for the night was cold. He had a chat with Dau in the saloon. It was, to him, just a routine affair. He did not get a glimpse of any hidden weapons, though he was not looking for anything of that nature. He was just a Customs' officer doing his job.

In the flats, the prisoners had settled down for the night. Melville-Evans was wondering what the harbour was called they had entered earlier, and of which he had made a sketch. After the incident of the aircraft swooping over the *Altmark*, the men were feeling subdued again. It seemed as if they were to be thwarted by the laws of neutrality.

The guards and the crew were doing their best to appear normal, but underneath it was clear that they were very nervous. The conditions had become much worse, and the captives were still having to make do with biscuits and water.

The ice had stopped the *Altmark* in her headlong flight up the fjord. The officers discussed the position and came to the conclusion that Dau would wait until the early hours of the morning and then make a dash for it.

"Well, there will be nothing doing tonight, lads," said Willis as he prepared to turn in. Others were inclined to agree and started to settle down on their makeshift beds.

Suddenly the lookout shouted: "Hold it, lads. I can see searchlights." There was a buzz of talk in the flats as this latest development was discussed. "What can it mean?" they asked each other. Were the searchlights being used by the Norwegians to check on the *Altmark*, or were the British in the fjord? The speculation continued, and then as nothing appeared to be happening the men made another attempt at settling down for the night.

"There they are again—the searchlights!" the lookout exclaimed. That was it. All pretence at sleep was abandoned as it was now clear that something important was afoot. Could rescue be at hand at last? It was.

Dau had been trying to rest, but was prevented from doing so by the nagging fear about the British warships that he knew were outside the fjord. He had given them the slip the first time, but could he do it again? The time must come when he would have to leave territorial waters, and then he would be at the mercy of the warships, unless he could get aircraft cover to give him a chance of completing the dash back to Germany.

He paced the bridge, and then all at once a searchlight stabbed the darkness of the fjord. "What is that?" He shot the question at First Officer Paulsen. "I do not know, Herr Kapitaen," Paulsen replied, "but there is a ship entering the fjord." The unknown ship stopped abeam of the torpedo-boats.

"Ask what ship and what nationality," rapped out Dau, now thoroughly alarmed. The Morse signal flashed out from the *Altmark*, but the intruder made no response.

"Order the crew to their stations," commanded Dau. The crew hurried to the positions to which they had been allotted in case of just such an emergency as this. Dau, Paulsen and Third Officer Schmidt took up stations on the bridge. Two other officers were on the forecastle, two on the poop-deck and two ready to lower the boats.

Another signal flashed out from the unknown ship. It read: "Do you require a tugboat? Take the pilot ladder on the port side."

Dau was by now both angry and alarmed. "Ask her again for her name and nationality." The signal was made, but the other ship once more failed to answer. Two minutes later, Dau was in no doubt as to the identity of the ship. The *Altmark* received the signal O.L., meaning "Heave to, or I start with my guns."

"It is the British," stormed Dau. "They have been ordered to capture my ship." Third Officer Schmidt remained with Dau, who ordered: "Slow ahead." The *Altmark* moved about eight hundred feet further into the fjord.

"The searchlights. The searchlights," Dau ordered. The *Altmark*'s searchlights played on the bridge of the ship, now revealed as the *Cossack*, with the object of blinding the officers on the bridge with the glare as well as to watch her movements. The destroyer passed the Norwegian torpedo-boats and approached the *Altmark*.

This was the moment everything had been leading up to. The issue would be settled one way or the other within the next few minutes. Churchill had in effect said: "Go in and get her if the Norwegians do not co-operate," and Captain (D) was doing just that. The grey hulk of the tanker grew closer.

"Right lads. Boarding party stand by." The order came on board the *Cossack* as the boarders mustered on the destroyer's forecastle. They were under orders to leap on to the *Altmark* as soon as the opportunity offered. Any man who missed his footing stood a good chance of being crushed between the two ships, or at best a ducking in the icy water. "Watch your step, lads," advised Petty Officer Atkins.

"Right, pilot. This looks like being a tricky one," said Captain Vian to his navigator, Lieutenant-Commander Hector MacLean. He also had thoughts about the 6-inch guns with which the *Altmark* was said to be armed, if the merchant captains' stories of flaps behind which guns were hidden were to be believed. The *Cossack* would be a sitting target if the *Altmark* were to blaze away with such weapons.

Vian shielded his eyes against the glare of the searchlights sweeping the *Cossack*. Dau had one last card up his sleeve. Ram this accursed Britisher. He ordered "Full astern," and it seemed that nothing could prevent the tanker crashing into the bow of the *Cossack*, but he had reckoned without the skill of the navigator, Lieutenant-Commander MacLean. His skill, coupled with the speed with which the engine-room responded, averted disaster. Instead, the *Altmark* grounded by the stern after Dau had also tried to force the destroyer ashore when boarding was taking place.

The moment of boarding was more in keeping with the days of sail than with a modern destroyer. Lieutenant-Commander Turner leapt six feet to land on the *Altmark* as the ships clashed together. Petty Officer Atkins followed, and for one breathtaking moment it looked as if he was going to fall between the vessels and be trapped between the plates. He managed to save himself with his hands, and as he hung there Lieutenant-Commander Turner managed to grab him and haul him aboard the *Altmark*. Quickly, the two made the vessels fast with a manilla hawser, from the *Cossack*'s forecastle to the tanker's quarter. The ships clashed together again and the rest of the boarders managed to get across. Of the forty-five forming the party, thirty-three succeeded in boarding.

The boarders fell into the agreed parties under their leaders and spread out to the various parts of the ship. It seemed that there was to be no trouble. No one had fired on them or tried to stop them as they scrambled aboard, but then a shot rang out. Gunner Smith, in charge of the after party, clutched his arm as he ran along an alleyway. He had been shot. Others of the boarders ducked as more shots came.

As the armed bluejackets advanced over the *Altmark*'s deck, Third Officer Schmidt was standing on the starboard wing of the bridge. "Herr Kapitaen," he called, "there are British marines [his term for armed sailors] aboard." He did not wait for a reply, but hurried to the engine-room telegraph and ordered "Full astern". He then ran to the port wing and threw overboard the confidential logbook, in its specially weighted bag, into an opening in the ice.

The crack of shots came from the poop-deck and members of the crew midships and aft began to lower boats on the port side. Schmidt dashed to the wheelhouse again and saw a British officer (Turner) swing the engine telegraph to "Stop". Schmidt jumped forward and swung it back to "Full astern." In the darkness, Turner called out: "Hands up", pointed his revolver at Schmidt's chest, and, with his free hand, put the telegraph back to "Stop." Three more of the boarding party flung themselves into the darkened wheelhouse and ordered: "Hands up."

Dau, still on the starboard wing, was concerning himself more with the manoeuvring of the ship rather than with the commotion going on around him. He was asked if he was the pilot, and when he agreed, he was left alone. Suddenly, there was a crash and a shudder as the tussle between the *Cossack* and the *Altmark* ended with the tanker wedged on the rocks.

Dau came in and told his officers not to worry as the ship had grounded. Hearing Dau speak in German came as a surprise to the boarders. They realized that they were looking at the captain. This was the Dau they had heard about. He was game to the last, it seemed. It was now that Sub-Lieutenant Craven's knowledge of German came in useful. He interrogated the officers. Dau and the prison officer, Weichert, agreed to go with them to the prisoners' flats.

While all this was in progress, there was some shooting and several Germans made for the shore. The Norwegian Customs officer also thought he was better out of it and scrambled down a rope and made for the shore over the ice. The Norwegian officer in command of the *Kjell* had not tried to board the *Altmark* but remained aboard the *Cossack*, which he left during the fighting.

On shore, people could hear the crack of shots and shouts and screams coming from the *Altmark*. Bullet marks were later to be found on the rocks beyond the road, and bloodstains in the snow and out to the edge of the ice.

The ice was not strong enough at certain points to hold the weight of a man and several fell through. Ten of the *Altmark*'s crew toppled into the water when a lifeboat capsized. The men in the water were crying out for help.

Germans were firing from the shore and were believed to be members of the *Graf Spee* guard placed on board the *Altmark* to guard the prisoners. Two Germans, fleeing to join those already on shore, were shot by the boarders but managed to reach the shore. But amid all the shooting and the panic there was still time for humanity to show through. Two of the *Cossack*'s officers jumped overboard to rescue one of the Germans who had fallen through the ice. With no thought for their own safety, Lieutenant-Commander Gerald Ormsby and Paymaster Lieutenant Edmund Burkitt jumped overboard. The man was hauled aboard the *Cossack*, but their efforts were in vain for he died. An identity disc gave his name as Hans Berndsen. His death was due to exposure. He had not been wounded.

The various sections of the boarding party were now reporting everything under control. Resistance had been overcome, and the question now was: where were the prisoners? Dau told his questioners: "The prisoners are downstairs, but you had better hurry. The ship is sinking now pretty fast." Sub-Lieutenant Craven was doing the questioning with his knowledge of German.

"Right, you stay here," Lieutenant-Commander Turner told the sub-lieutenant. "I'll go with these two." He indicated Dau and the prison officer, who had agreed to show him the prisoners' quarters.

Sub-Lieutenant Craven remained on the bridge with two guards, while the *Cossack*'s first lieutenant went with a sentry and the two Germans to see to the release of the prisoners.

The noise of the shooting had been heard by the prisoners, and they were fully alert to the fact that an attempt was being made to rescue them. Bullets slammed into the hatch door, and the lookout abandoned his place at the spyhole. There was no sense at this late stage in falling victim to a bullet, especially if it came from a friendly source.

It was not a simple task to release the prisoners. Lieutenant-Commander Turner found that the German sentries had made off with the keys. The door had also been so tightly bound with wire during the time the prisoners were trying to attract the attention of the Norwegians that it took about ten minutes to open.

Finally, the door was flung back and the men below heard a voice shout: "Are there any Englishmen down there?" The great response of "Yes; we're all English" left no doubt that there were. "Then come on up. The Navy's here!" the voice commanded. Those words, "The Navy's here", were words the captives would never forget as long as they lived. They were to echo around the world, but in that moment they were words only for the ears of men who had been waiting and praying for so long for the appearance of the Navy.

They had boarded in the old seadog tradition and were proving that though ships may change, the men of the Royal Navy had no equal when it came to the point. The men of the Merchant Navy might not have the discipline of the men of the Navy, but there was no mad rush when the way to freedom was clear. Everything had been prepared for the time when they would have to make a quick exit from the ship. The agreed procedure was followed.

George King, second engineer of the *Doric Star*, who had been keeping watch, took charge and ensured an orderly exit from the three decks, the men from the lower deck being sent up first. Dau and Lieutenant "Babyface" Schmidt, the officer in charge of the guard, were at the top under guard when King clambered out, and they shook hands with him. King had to use his hands in another way when an armed German got in his way as the prisoners left the hatch. The man had a revolver, and to King it seemed a situation that brooked no delay. He hit out with his fist and knocked the German cold.

Wally Wells, seventh engineer of the *Tairoa*, hauled himself on deck and was surprised at the smallness of the fjord, and the immensity of the surrounding mountains. It was bright moonlight, and to him the snow-covered slopes and ice-covered fjord seemed to have been copied from a Christmas card. Melville-Evans also gazed in wonderment at the scene, and his fellow officer from the *Doric Star*, Archibald Willis, was admiring the surroundings with an artistic eye.

As the prisoners mustered on deck, Lieutenant-Commander Turner told them that Dau had stated that the *Altmark* was set to blow up in an hour and asked them to transfer to the *Cossack* as quickly as they could. The destroyer returned alongside the tanker and Lieutenant-Commander Turner shouted across to Captain Vian that he would "send the Englishmen over first and then the Germans". Captain Vian stated that he "did not want the Germans".

The explosion scare arose when several of the *Altmark*'s officers asked to be allowed to don lifejackets. When this was refused they said Dau had set explosive charges, but Dau could not be questioned as he was then concerned with the freeing of the prisoners. Captain Vian continued with the embarking of the men freed from the *Altmark*, having decided to disregard the message received about the charges, believing its import improbable.

A check was made of the freed prisoners for disease, but all were clear except for one leper. The 6-inch guns the *Altmark* was said to have been carrying were not found.

Dr Tyrolt, the *Altmark*'s doctor, forgot all about his fear of being captured as he set about treating the wound of Gunner Smith. Tyrolt was the first man to reach him and began immediately to apply a dressing. It was only at the point of a bayonet that Tyrolt could be made to leave Smith. When he did arrive on deck some shots were fired at him, but prisoners already on the deck of *Cossack* shouted: "Don't shoot—that's the German doctor." A lot of the prisoners said goodbye to him before they boarded the destroyer.

The closing moments of the boarding episode saw surprising scenes between the freed prisoners and their former captors. There were handshakes and good wishes. Captain Starr, master of the *Tairoa*, and Captain Brown, of the *Huntsman*, shared a cabin on board the *Altmark*. Captain Starr was among those who said goodbye to Dr Tyrolt. They shook hands and Tyrolt commented, "It is the fortune of war."

Captain Brown, who had collected a few of his belongings, including his best suit, before the boarding because he had a feeling that something was going to happen, was running along after learning that charges had been set when he heard his name called. Shots were still whistling through the air, but Captain Brown stopped. The man who had called to him was a German electrician who had had the job of screwing up the portholes of the two captains' cabin and they had become quite friendly.

The German had been shot and was already weak from loss of blood. He had apparently told the boarding party that there were two captains in a cabin aft. The German could speak only a little English, but Captain Brown shook hands with him and expressed the wish that everything would turn out all right.

It was now almost midnight and time to be moving. The Germans were waiting on the forecastle deck of the *Altmark* expecting at any moment to be ordered to go aboard the *Cossack*, but no such order came. The destroyer let go her ropes and began to edge her way out of the fjord past the torpedo-boats and to the open sea. "They are not taking us with them," said First Officer Paulsen, expressing the surprise they all felt at this turn of events.

There was, however, no time to ponder. They had to see to the dead and wounded. Some eighteen men were picked up out of the water, wrapped in blankets and given hot tea. One man died after attempts to revive him failed. Third Officer Schmidt searched the decks for wounded men and found the fourth engineer and one steward on the aft boatdeck. Both were badly wounded. Other severely wounded men were found on the other side of the ship. All the wounded were taken to the ship's hospital and Dr Tyrolt began operating. Third Officer Schmidt gave him a hand, and later a Norwegian doctor came aboard and helped.

There were six dead: Stender, Bremer, Steffen, all stewards; Rothe, greaser; Schurmann, a guard; and Meyer. Missing was Berndsen (the man whom the two officers from the *Cossack* had jumped into the sea to rescue). Those wounded were: Claussen, Augustin, Richartz, Schuler and Horst. The inclusion of Bernsden brought the total dead to seven. Most of the casualties had been shot when they tried to lower a boat or to escape on shore.

(The charge was made that dum-dum bullets were used because of the severe nature of the wounds, but in later years it was agreed that the wounds gave this appearance because they were inflicted at short range.)

"We are still missing some men, Herr Kapitaen," First Officer Paulsen told Dau. Some were still on shore. Twenty were missing, but nineteen returned after staying with Norwegian families. But the remaining missing man never did turn up, and the conclusion was drawn that he had drowned in the general scramble as men fled across the ice or jumped into the water.

As the Germans were counting the cost of their encounter with the

Royal Navy, the *Cossack* was heading for Leith in triumph, reporting 299 prisoners on board, much to the relief of the First Sea Lord, Admiral Sir Dudley Pound, and Winston Churchill, First Lord of the Admiralty. Both had been waiting anxiously in the Admiralty War Room and keeping abreast of developments. It seemed that Churchill, the old warhorse, had pulled it off again with his signal to Captain Vian. The diplomatic row was yet to come.

A message was despatched from the Admiralty to Captain (D). It read: "Well done, *Cossack.*"

The Navy dealt a double blow against the Germans that night, for the *Ivanhoe* was on patrol outside Jossingfjord with the *Intrepid* when she received an order to investigate a merchant ship. This was the German iron-ore ship *Baldur. Ivanhoe* put a couple of shots across her bows. The crew scuttled their ship and took to the boats, being picked up by the *Ivanhoe* and the *Intrepid.* The flotilla had reason to be in good spirits as they set course for home.

There was little room to spare in the wartime destroyers at the best of times, but with almost three hundred extra men on board, accommodation in the *Cossack* was stretched to the limit. Nevertheless the crew did the best with the limited facilities at their disposal. Each man soon had something to eat and drink. The fifty-five officers from the merchant ships were put in the wardroom and were given a warm welcome. They were soon telling the few officers of the *Cossack* who had time to listen of their experiences in the *Graf Spee* and the *Altmark.*

Melville-Evans, who had charted the route of the *Altmark* from the South Atlantic and also made a sketch of the harbour in which the *Altmark* had entered off Norway, was summoned to the presence of the captain, Vian, to elaborate on them. Churchill had sent them, said Captain Vian. The captain later addressed the men who a short time before had been prisoners in the *Altmark,* and told them how pleased they were that they were now free. "He's a topper," Melville-Evans commented to Wally Wells.

The third officer of the *Doric Star* was not alone in his admiration of the man who had snatched them almost from the jaws of a prison camp, and who, along with others of his men, was to be decorated. (Both Captain Vian and Lieutenant-Commander Turner were awarded the D.S.O.) Men who had at one time given up hope of ever being rescued were now full of praise for the Navy. They talked and talked and were almost too excited to sleep, but in the end sheer exhaustion drove them to bed down where they could and snatch some sleep as the destroyer made for Leith.

Soon it was time to get up again, and the former prisoners who had been living on biscuits and water when the *Altmark* had been taking drastic measures to keep the presence of the captives secret, now fell to with a will on a breakfast of porridge, bacon and eggs, fruit, toast and marmalade. There was also a three-course lunch that would have done credit to many a restaurant. The food and the serving of it was a tribute to the stewards and the cook. They waited on the released officers cheerfully and without complaint. Their work did not go unnoticed by Captain Vian.

Wally Wells felt compelled to comment on the contrast with the conditions in the *Graf Spee*, where the prisoners had been given only cold coffee and thick soup. There had been only 180 prisoners in the pocket battleship compared to the 299 in the *Cossack* with her cramped conditions and limited facilities.

The *Cossack* had made all speed possible, for she did not want to become a target for German aircraft bent on revenge after the affair in the fjord. The sound of aircraft engines was heard just after daybreak, but it was a flight of R.A.F. aircraft who were to provide an escort to Leith.

There was a scare when the aircraft spotted mines ahead. The *Cossack*, in the lead, immediately fell behind and the escort took the lead to ensure that the rescued men should be in the least danger. One of the aircraft dived low and, with a burst of gunfire, sank one mine. One of the escorting destroyers sank three others with gunfire.

The news of the release of the prisoners from the *Altmark* had gone ahead. As it was feared that they would be in poor condition after their ordeal in the "hell-ship", the authorities had made arrangements for the *Cossack* to be met with ambulances and ambulance personnel and for their reception in hospitals for decontamination, bathing and feeding. The authorities expected stretcher cases and men suffering from malnutrition after their experiences in the tanker.

Officials were prepared for anything except for what they did see as H.M.S. *Cossack* berthed at Leith at 1545 hours on that never-to-be-forgotten day, 17th February 1940. They saw men crowded on the decks of the destroyer cheering and waving to those on the quayside. They wore old clothes, caps and mufflers, but beneath their bedraggled appearance there was a spirit that months of captivity had not subdued.

The men were nevertheless grateful that the authorities should have been so thoughtful as to provide these facilities. They were also thankful that they did not need them. The occasion was a field day for the Press and they gave the story the full treatment, and, it must be admitted, it was a good one, having all the ingredients to capture the public's attention. It was not long before the newspapers were carrying stories with headlines such as: "Rescued men tell horrors of *Altmark*", "Mother's tears, sweetheart's caress. Men from dead knock at door".

The "hell-ship" aspect gained so much ground that when the authorities interviewed survivors the men themselves were saying that they felt the reports of their treatment had been exaggerated. The official interviews gave the Admiralty the first real accounts of conditions in the *Altmark*, apart from those given by those officers released in Montevideo, and of what had occurred on passage along the Norwegian coast before the arrival of the Navy.

One important witness was Melville-Evans. He had been busy tracking the *Altmark*, but the Admiralty also wanted to know about the harbour he had sketched and, more important, where it was. The *Doric Star*'s "third" found himself answering a lot of questions in London and making a sworn statement.

He said the *Altmark* sailed straight up the harbour, which had a town at the back of it. He noticed this because he was on watch at the lookout hole until midnight. The *Altmark* sailed straight up the harbour towards the quay, but did not anchor. About thirty minutes later, a vessel was heard coming alongside which must have been as big as a tug, judging by the force of impact and the crunching noise. He observed features of the town and a cement quay long enough to take the *Altmark*.

The town seemed to be of some size with very high ground behind it. There was also a factory at the back of the town. On the starboard side of the entrance there was a rock formation "consisting of four hills of a sugar-loaf shape". Some of the prisoners felt there was little doubt that the place was Bergen.

One of those who thought the same as Melville-Evans was Harold Gandy, chief steward of the *Doric Star*, whose home was in Southampton. He also made a sworn statement. The *Altmark* had lingered in fjords—in one of which there was a canning factory on the port side—and then, after leaving the open sea, had arrived at the harbour described by the *Doric Star*'s third officer. The lights of the town were quite visible, and from Melville-Evans's description he was certain that it was Bergen. He had been familiar with the Norwegian coast and its ports for twelve years, Harold Gandy added by way of emphasis.

Had the *Altmark* been in Bergen Harbour or not? A secret message was sent to the British Consul in Bergen asking if he could identify a harbour similar to that described by the two Merchant Navy officers in their sworn statements. Was there also a canning factory on the port side of Sognefjord going in? An urgent reply was requested.

The reply came the following day, saying that local shipping circles and pilots tentatively identified the town as Haugesund, but the description did not tally in every respect, especially the omission of a new bridge to the mainland. Sugar loaf hills were characteristic of the Lofoten Islands. There was a small crab-packing plant on the port side of the southern entrance to Sognefjord.

So that was that. For years afterwards Melville-Evans still pondered the question as to which harbour the *Altmark* had entered, and enter one it had for he had the sketch to prove it as well as the opinions of his shipmates. The Norwegian Admiral had also informed the British Consul in Bergen on 17th February that the *Altmark* did not enter the port of Bergen.

The Germans were having their problems as well. They buried their dead in the cemetery in the village of Sogndal, but even this did not pass without warlike overtones. A report from the British Legation, Oslo, to the Foreign Secretary, Lord Halifax, stated that the funeral had been the setting for some strong language. The German Minister in Oslo, Dr Brauer, made a speech in which he was reported to have said: "These comrades of ours met their death at the hands of murderers." The *Altmark* was "an unarmed merchant ship which had simply been fetching oil and provisions for its country and people".

A Norwegian Navy officer was also stated to have weighed in by speaking of "the wrath which this violation of Norwegian neutrality has roused in the entire Norwegian people". Dau was also apparently in full flow and here made the charge that dum-dum bullets had been used by bluejackets.

The German propaganda machine was quick off the mark. Men from the Propaganda Ministry in Berlin flew in by plane to Jossingfjord. Dau was interviewed and so also was Chief Officer Paulsen. The British came in for strong criticism, and the boarders were accused of having stolen the captain's fountain pen.

The allegations of looting were taken seriously by the Admiralty, and this led to a personal minute from Churchill, as First Lord, in which he stated he had seen that charges of looting had been made in the German Press. It had come to his notice that property belonging to the captain of the *Altmark*, a watch, chronometer and Iron Cross, had been stolen and was in the hands of some of the sailors as souvenirs. Anything of this kind must be stopped with the utmost strictness, he ordered.

A report subsequently submitted by Lieutenant-Commander Turner said that looting might have occurred, but that it must have been on a very small scale and by very few individuals. The released prisoners were mostly concerned in getting their scanty belongings and preparing to transfer to the *Cossack*. He was certain that the boarding party did not do any looting. They were, in any case, far too busy.

Other reports were also made. The items that were retrieved were an automatic pistol and loading clips, picked up by one of the prisoners, a notice taken from the prisoners' quarters, a spent German cartridge case and a German seaman's identity book.

It was felt that there was no evidence to show that ratings took part in looting. Articles that had been removed were apparently handed in and were not the type of article likely to be taken if looting was the intention.

The *Altmark* affair was, of course, an excellent opportunity for both the British and Germans to extract the fullest propaganda value from the incident in the days before television. Today there would have been television crews flying in and interviewing local inhabitants, and the world would have been seeing the event in their front rooms almost as it happened. In those days, in that remote Norwegian fjord, it was a different matter.

The fighting was given a lot of publicity, as were the conditions in the *Altmark*, leading to the hell-ship claim, but what seemed to escape notice were the little acts of kindness shown by the Norwegians towards men who were in a very short time to be their enemies also, following the invasion of Norway by Germany. The community around Jossingfjord was a peaceful one and life went on calmly with little to disturb their orderly routine—until the *Altmark* entered the fjord with the British snapping at her heels. Even with the *Altmark*'s arrival, the Norwegian inhabitants did not suspect that they were to be involved in an event that was to ensure Jossingfjord a place in the history books and would be remembered whenever men discussed what was to be termed "The *Altmark* affair".

Customs' officer Egaas went to see if he could help after the *Cossack* had departed, and met Chief Officer Paulsen out looking for men who had fled. A German was lying hurt in a ditch, and another was dead on the road. Many of the Germans were made welcome by local people who provided warmth and hot drinks.

A fisherman called Elliassen saw the *Altmark* in the fjord, but as he had had a hard day went to bed without concerning himself so much about the tanker. He was asleep when the sound of shooting awoke him. He lay there wondering what was happening and heard screams and shouting mingled with the crack of the shots. Half an hour later, when there seemed to be no more shooting, he pulled on some clothes and went outside. The *Cossack* had gone. There were bloodstains in the snow.

Lensman Claus told of finding bullet marks in the rocks beyond the road, and there were similar marks on a factory wall.

A chauffeur by the name of Arstad described driving to Jossinghavn, where he saw searchlights and heard the sound of shots. He also saw life-belts lying on the road.

A teacher, Lars Dahl, saw the whole episode, from the arrival of the *Altmark* until the boarding. He afterwards saw Germans running towards him who were soaked through.

The Norwegians, giving evidence at an official inquiry in Egersund, spoke of bloodstains in the snow. Germans were found wandering about and taken in for shelter and warmth and the wounded to have their wounds tended. One man had been hit three times. The following day, a Norwegian followed bloodstains down to the road and over the ice towards the *Altmark*.

The Norwegians told of their experiences in simple language. They lived a simple life and wished only to be left in peace to go about their work. They had been thrown into a situation that was not of their making, and in offering aid to the Germans had done only what they would have done for the British, or for any other seamen in a similar situation. They were not concerned that British and German observers were present at the inquiry. It was no affair of theirs. They would be glad when the *Altmark* was repaired and able to put to sea again. They would then also be free of the British aircraft that came over keeping an eye on the tanker that was now fair game for any lurking British submarine or aircraft once she regained the open sea.

So, in due time, life was to return to normal in the fjord where 299 British seamen found freedom and seven Germans death. The snow was to fall again and cover the marks of violence and the cleansing sea to wash away the blood.

12

The Log Is Closed

The *Altmark* affair did not end with the boarding of the tanker in Jossingfjord. Rather was it the signal for a new flutter of diplomatic activity and for recrimination among the Norwegians. The British came in for strong criticism from both the Germans and the Norwegians. The Germans, after invading Norway, even went to the extent of erecting a signboard on the shore of Jossingfjord. Inscribed on the board were the words: "Here on the 16th February 1940, the *Altmark* was set upon by a British sea pirate."

It did not take long for the Norwegians to act. On the same day as the liberated prisoners arrived in Britain, the Norwegian Ministry of Foreign Affairs was the setting for a meeting. The First Sea Lord, Admiral Diesen, was one of those who attended. The events of the previous evening were discussed at length. It was felt that the matter could not be let pass. The conclusion was reached that a strong protest must be lodged against this violation of Norwegian neutrality. The Germans, too, were soon to make a protest, their envoy pressing for the Norwegians to lodge a strong complaint with the British Government.

The British Envoy, Sir Cecil Dormer, was summoned by the Prime Minister, Mr Nygaardsvold. The Prime Minister told Sir Cecil that the incident had caused great distress to the Norwegians. They could not understand why the British should act in such a manner. He made it plain that his country did not like this action that had taken place in their own backyard, as it were.

It was a sticky interview and the Norwegians wanted a full apology. Sir Cecil fenced and pointed out that the *Altmark* had used her wireless while in territorial waters. He asked whether the *Altmark* had been arrested for this, but was told that the Norwegian Government had not had any report of this contravention of the regulations.

The Norwegians were not to be moved by this argument over the radio transmission. To them, it was merely obscuring the real issue, which was that the British Navy should not have violated Norwegian neutrality. The British Envoy stuck to the point that the Norwegians should have arrested the *Altmark* for using her wireless. It was also the Norwegian view that the *Altmark*, even with prisoners on board, would have been entitled to sail through territorial waters.

Naturally, the Germans were making all the capital they could out of the incident. They had been humiliated and were to see the British snatch a brilliant propaganda victory from the episode once the Press got to work on it. The Germans claimed that the *Altmark* had not been offered enough protection. Berlin was kept fully acquainted with the facts by the German Envoy, Dr Gurt Brauer, who was also told in mitigation by the Norwegians that their torpedo-boats could not in all fairness have been expected to do battle with the British destroyers.

In London, while Churchill, as First Lord of the Admiralty, was in high glee at the outcome of the rescue attempt, the note of protest landed on the desk of the Foreign Secretary, Lord Halifax. The Norwegian Government, in setting out their protest, said the freed prisoners should be sent back to Norway. Lord Halifax was having none of this, making it clear to the Norwegian Minister in London, Mr Colban, that the British Government could not return the prisoners. There again arose the question of whether the *Altmark* had been inspected in a proper manner. Lord Halifax contended that the Norwegians had not done this properly. In the circumstances, it was felt, Lord Halifax told Mr Colban, that the British had acted in the correct manner and the outcome had justified their action.

Whatever Norway felt—and the point was made that, according to international law, it was normal for belligerent powers occasionally to take prisoners through neutral waters—the British were overjoyed at the success of the Royal Navy. They did not care whether or not Norwegian neutrality rights had been infringed. The Prime Minister, Neville Chamberlain, also rubbed salt into Norway's wounds with a statement in Parliament expressing satisfaction at the action of the Royal Navy.

If Parliament was behind the British Government in this action, then the Norwegian Parliament was also behind the Norwegian Government in the steps they had taken. They had heard a statement that the *Altmark* had to be classed with warships and therefore should not be searched. The fact was that both countries considered themselves in the right. The only thing the Norwegians would admit was that it was an error of judgement to have permitted the tanker to sail through the Bergen Defended Area. It was also felt that this did not give the British *carte blanche* to intercept the supply ship. A factor from the British point of view was that time was not on their side. The Royal Navy had to go in and do the job quickly if they were to avoid the risk of attack by German aircraft. The cover of darkness was essential in the final stages of the operation.

There is one point that does not appear to have been considered. What if the British had taken Dau, his crew and the guards with them when they steamed out of Jossingfjord? The urgency of the need to get clear as quickly as possible seems to have been the deciding factor. There were some among the boarding party from the *Cossack* who seemed to think that the Germans would be sent across to the *Cossack* until the order was given to send only the released prisoners. In other less urgent circumstances, dawn might well have found the Norwegians confronted with a tanker wedged on the rocks devoid of both crew and prisoners. It is not hard to imagine the diplomatic row that would then have ensued.

The Germans themselves were no less surprised at being left on the deck of the *Altmark* gazing at the departing *Cossack* and hardly able to believe their luck. Walter Schmidt was annoyed that some personal belongings, including a photograph of his wife, had been taken by souvenir hunters among the boarding party, but considered himself lucky to be alive. The Germans were now free to bury their dead, and to see to what extent the *Altmark* was damaged before considering resuming the voyage to Germany minus the prisoners.

The Norwegian Government might well have justified their stance, insisting they had done all they could in ascertaining the true role of the *Altmark*, and soothing the hurt pride of the Germans as the British Navy literally kicked them in the jackboot, but there remained individual Norwegians who were not entirely satisfied with the manner in which their country had handled the situation. The whole affair was a blow to their pride.

One of these was Captain Sigurd S. Arstad, who was serving in Bergen. He made his views known in a letter to his father, Morten Arstad, a dentist in Stavanger.

Captain Arstad described to his father how the *Altmark* first arrived in Norwegian waters and how the *Trygg* was ordered to inspect the tanker and report to him. He received a short telegram saying the inspection had been done. Captain Arstad and his officers studied their files and learned that according to English newspapers the

Altmark had been supply ship to the *Admiral Graf Spee* and carried about 400 British prisoners.

The Norwegian Navy officer wanted to know to what extent the inspection had been carried out and tried to contact the *Trygg* by wireless. He found that it was impossible to contact the *Trygg* in this way and had to wait until she came into her station at Kristiandsund, and then spoke to her captain by telephone. The conversation disclosed the fact that the inspection had not been made according to the orders of the Commanding Admiral. It appeared that the *Altmark*'s papers had only been checked and that no investigation had been made as to what armament she carried. The vessel was flying the state flag.

Captain Arstad went on to describe the intervention of the *Garm*, the halting of the *Altmark* and the boarding by Captain Stamso. He wrote: "The prisoners down below were whistling through their fingers S.O.S. and were waving through the portholes. All the steam-winches were then started on *Altmark* to make a lot of noise, and the portholes were closed."

Referring to the use of the *Altmark*'s wireless while in Norwegian waters, the letter goes on: "We afterwards learned that there had been lots of telegrams running between *Altmark* to Germany, Germany to the German Embassy in Oslo, and from there to *Altmark*."

The legation in Oslo also entered the affair, he wrote, and Rear-Admiral Tank-Nielsen was ordered immediately to telephone the Kommanderende Admiral in Oslo. The Kommanderende Admiral was not pleased at the situation and used some hard words on the telephone and said the *Altmark* should be permitted to go through the Norwegian Navy Harbour without inspection, "in spite of our great suspicion that the ship's armament was so great that it had to be considered as offensive armament. The ship should go through without inspection. This is, of course, also seen by the English airplanes".

The letter continued:

> If our standpoint had been adhered to, the ship would probably have been attacked outside Norwegian territorial waters, and she would probably have fled in again. This would have meant that we could intern the ship and free the prisoners, without anybody saying that Norway had not followed international law.
>
> The situation as of now is that Norway has permitted an auxiliary cruiser

to use Norwegian waters and Navy Harbour. It is quite clear that if a ship, which is a man-of-war, but camouflaged as a cargo ship, shall be allowed to use the Norwegian coast, then we have *rowed* ourself too far out.

Don't misunderstand me. I do not sympathize with the way the English behaved, but we had first committed a great blunder. The only correct conclusion ought to be that the Commanding Admiral, together with our Foreign Minister, ought to go.

What is still sadder is that this is the No 2 affair of a similar type. We also had earlier a German ship which was camouflaged in the same way, which they let go, and this is of course also known by the English.

The *Altmark* was at that time (the letter was dated Bergen, 20th February 1940), wrote Captain Sigurd, lying in First District (Southern Norway) and he did not know what inspection had been carried out. "If," he went on, "it turns out that it is correct what the Englishmen say, that the armament is of offensive character—she is supposed to have three 6-inch cannons—then I have great difficulty in understanding how our Foreign Office can avoid interning the ship."

These were the views of a man who was a true patriot. For later that year, after the German occupation of Norway, Captain Arstad fled with his family in a fishing-boat to England, where he served with the Norwegian Navy throughout the war, mostly in headquarters, and returned home at the end of the war. He died in 1965.

The Norwegians were also not inclined to rush to the aid of the Germans stranded with the *Altmark* in Jossingfjord. It was essential that they had the services of two Norwegian pilots if the *Altmark* were to be navigated out of the fjord and on the next stage of her voyage.

There was no rush to take on the job. Oscar Olsen, a pilot in the Stavanger area since 1923, received a telephone call from the master pilot in Oslo telling him that the *Altmark* was to be transferred to Horten (the Norwegian Naval base near Oslo). Two pilots were needed for the task and he, Olsen was told, had been chosen as one of them. The other was a colleague from Bergen, also called Olsen.

Oscar Olsen was not pleased at the prospect, being well informed on the political implications of the affair. He was reluctant to take on the job and said as much to the master pilot, saying he would not go unless he was given a firm order. The master pilot told him: "It is a command."

Olsen had then no choice but to obey. The following morning he was joined by the pilot from Bergen and together they went down to Jossingfjord.

The British were still keeping an eye on the *Altmark* as each day at noon an aircraft flew over the fjord. The Germans also feared that a British submarine would sink the *Altmark* when she was afloat again. They worked feverishly to get the tanker in something like seaworthiness. They began by trimming the water ballast and freed the ship from the rocks and moved her about 250 feet by means of an anchor chain. With the ship once more afloat, the *Altmark*'s diver went down to examine the rudder and propellers. He found that the rudder was badly damaged and both propellers had each lost one blade and the others were bent.

The next problem was that of the engines. They had been under great strain during the final moments in the fjord before the *Cossack* had taken command of the situation. Would they be in working order? First Engineer Schleusner listened anxiously as the engines were started up and run very carefully. Schleusner breathed with relief as they began to run smoothly. The shafts were apparently undamaged.

That was the condition in which Oscar Olsen and his colleague found the *Altmark* when they arrived at Jossingfjord. They were faced with the problem of getting the tanker to Horten without use of the rudder. The ship had to be manoeuvred by manipulating the motors and the propellers. It proved a difficult task, but gradually they made progress. Two Norwegian tugs helped to manoeuvre the *Altmark* out of the narrow entrance to the fjord before she continued her voyage in territorial waters. Oscar Olsen and the other pilot were kept busy as every two or three minutes a manoeuvre was made with one of the engines, from "stop" to "half-a-head" and "slow astern" to keep the tanker on the right course.

All the crew wore lifejackets as they expected to be attacked by a British submarine. The tanker made a speed of eleven knots. Two Norwegian warships were guiding the *Altmark* on her trip to Horten, and were supposed to be covering her on the starboard side, but whatever the supply ship's difficulties she seemed faster than the escorts and soon left them behind. But the Norwegians were still in charge of the situation, for, in addition to the pilots, Norwegian soldiers were on board as guards.

As the *Altmark* sailed towards Horten, Oscar Olsen had the opportunity to study Dau, whom he found a strong character and devoted to Hitler. It was with a show of pride that Dau informed the pilots that his son also was a sea officer, being in charge of a submarine. Dau lamented that because of his age he himself was prevented from serving in the submarine service. The *Altmark* reached Horten without any special difficulty having occurred on passage from Jossingfjord. Oscar Olsen left the *Altmark* with the thought that at least he had done his duty, even if that duty was not of his choosing.

There were more discussions between the German and Norwegian Governments before the *Altmark* was allowed to leave and sail for Germany. A large German tugboat, the *Albatross*, was sent out to meet the *Altmark* and stay with her as protection against possible submarine attack. The *Altmark* arrived at Kiel on 28th March 1940, to a warm welcome. The crew were given three weeks' leave, and were fêted and toasted after their long and eventful voyage that had seen them leave some of their comrades behind in Norway, buried in a little cemetery.

Third Officer Schmidt stayed with the *Altmark* until August 1940, afterwards going to Hamburg to take his master's certificate. In 1941, he became chief officer and, in 1943, master of several German Navy icebreakers and salvage ships, in which he sailed the English Channel, along the Norwegian coast and in the Baltic. It was while in the Baltic that he saved three Canadians and five Americans from the icy water after their aircraft was shot down.

Two days after the war in Europe ended, he sailed his ship into Copenhagen. It was then that the shadow of the *Altmark* fell across him. For from August 1945 until March 1946 he was imprisoned in a special prisoners' camp for having been third officer in the *Altmark* and, it was alleged, treating the prisoners badly.

Walter Schmidt knew in his heart that he had not treated prisoners badly, and, in fact, had had very little to do with them, being a deck officer. He was worried, nevertheless, knowing that many of his fellow countrymen faced trial for their conduct in the war. It was a relief, therefore, when a British colonel sent for him at the end of March and told him he was free to go because he was not the man for whom they were searching.

He had lost much weight owing to the poor food in the camp, but this was nothing to being free again. His first thought was to go home, which was now in the Russian Zone. He crossed into the zone under cover of darkness and was relieved to find his wife safe and well.

The war had cost him the best years of his life, and he resolved that his family would learn how other people lived outside Germany. His three children, after they grew up, were to stay with families in England, America, France and South America and to work in those countries.

There was another upheaval for the Schmidt family in 1955 when they fled across the border from East Germany to freedom in the West. Captain Schmidt captained cargo ships, tankers and supertankers before retiring in July 1976 after forty-six years at sea. He and his wife now live in Lübeck, West Germany.

So the members of the *Altmark* who had taken part in the historic voyage went their various ways. Dr Tyrolt, the cheerful doctor who became a popular figure in the prisoners' flats and who showed courage as the *Cossack* boarding party stormed the *Altmark*, seems to have vanished without trace. Did he survive the war and leave a devastated Germany to go on yet another adventure to add a further chapter to an already interesting and, at times, exciting life?

Chief Officer Paulsen, First Engineer Schleusner, Second Officers Rummler and Garte, Schwill, the cook, Treibel, the baker, Becker, the carpenter . . . all played their part in the *Altmark* story.

But what of Kapitaen Dau? He was, in the beginning, the master of just another supply ship and would no doubt have seen out the war in this or similar capacity without attracting attention. He was a man thrown into the limelight by circumstances over which he had no control. The *Altmark* earned the title of "hell-ship", which looks good in newspaper headlines and helps fuel a nation's propaganda, but the state of health of the prisoners when they arrived at Leith rather gave the lie to this. There had been no brutality, but conditions were hard and could have been little else when 300 prisoners had to be accommodated at short notice.

The term "hell-ship" brings to mind a picture of men being brutally treated and many dying. This was not the case. Dau, it has been generally agreed, was a Nazi and keen follower of Hitler, but was he a "monster" as one description had it? The truth is probably that he was strict, in keeping with the old Imperial German Navy tradition and, as a supporter of Hitler, was pleased that the British, at that stage, were suffering many defeats. He hectored the prisoners and insisted that they be dealt with strictly, but generally he seems to have coped as best he could. A tanker on the high seas suddenly having to take on the role of a floating prison cannot be compared with a recognized prisoner-of-war camp with its commandant, proper guards and rules and regulations.

Dau made the claim to his third officer, Walter Schmidt, that some of the prisoners shook him by the hand after they scrambled on the *Altmark*'s deck following their release by the *Cossack*, as many of them did with Dr Tyrolt, which the third officer saw for himself.

Dau can no longer defend himself, for he took his own life when Germany surrendered in May 1945, leaving a family to mourn him. Ironically, both the captains of the principal ships involved in the *Altmark* affair had now died by their own hand, Langsdorff shooting himself after the scuttling of the *Graf Spee*, and Dau committing suicide when his beloved Fatherland lost the war.

The *Altmark*, which had been the subject of such headlines as "Hell-ship caught" and "Hand-to-hand fight in Nazi prison ship", was herself long gone.

She was renamed *Uckermark*, and under this name sailed as a supply ship to the German armed merchant cruiser *Thor*. The vessels were alongside each other at Yokohama, Japan, on 30th November 1942, when the *Uckermark* was torn by explosions. Both ships were destroyed and many of the *Uckermark*'s crew killed. Work was being carried out to the *Uckermark*'s oil tanks at the time and a spark resulting from this was believed to be the cause of the disaster. The *Altmark* had made headlines during her short life and had now gone out in a final blaze of glory.

It was a sad moment for Third Officer Schmidt and other former members of the crew when they learned the news. The *Altmark* was a ship that would always have a special place in their memories. She had had a useful career after returning to Germany following the Jossingfjord incident, and being refitted.

March 1941 found her at sea sharing in the Battle of the Atlantic as *Uckermark* by helping to supply the *Scharnhorst* and *Gneisenau* in their onslaught on the convoys. She was in St Nazaire for a year and survived the famous St Nazaire raid.

Refitted again, she set sail in the summer of 1942 with the object of reaching the Far East, but was unable to get past the British blockade, and it was a month later before she was able to do so. She had on board two Arado seaplanes for the *Thor*. In due course, she arrived at Yokohama. There the *Uckermark* and *Thor*, side by side, presented a fine excuse for a celebration. It was decided that a lunch should be held on board *Thor* to which German and Japanese journalists should be invited. It was after lunch that the explosion occurred. There was a general rush to escape from both doomed ships, and some of those who jumped into the water were caught up in the burning oil that spread across the surface.

It seemed that the *Uckermark*, or *Altmark*, was fated to have honour snatched from her at the last moment. As the *Altmark*, she had narrowly missed reaching Germany with her prisoners, with the attendant celebrations, and now, as the *Uckermark*, had been deprived of her value as a means of propaganda by the disastrous explosion. The log of the *Altmark*/*Uckermark* was finally closed.

The *Altmark* and the *Graf Spee* both shared violent ends, though the *Graf Spee*'s had been inflicted deliberately on the orders of her captain. Yet the memory of the pocket battleship has not been allowed to die. When the fortieth anniversary of the Battle of the River Plate fell in December 1979, some of those who served in the *Graf Spee* paid their own special tribute to her memory and to those of her crew who died in the battle.

More than a hundred survivors of the Battle of the River Plate gathered in Buenos Aires to honour the dead and relive in memory the battle and its aftermath. Thirty of the survivors were from West Germany, eighteen were veterans of the cruiser *Achilles* from New Zealand and ten were Britons who had served in the cruisers *Ajax* and *Exeter*. They joined former members of the crew of the *Graf Spee* now settled in Argentina and Uruguay. They all took part in a wreath-laying ceremony in Buenos Aires, along with the West German, British and New Zealand ambassadors. Later, the survivors went to Montevideo to visit the British and German cemeteries and to gaze across the waters of the River Plate at the buoy that marks the spot where the pocket battleship ended her career.

It seemed that almost every ship linked with the *Altmark* affair was destined to end her life violently. The *Graf Spee* had sunk her prizes and she herself had been blown up in the final ignominy of scuttling. H.M.S. *Cossack* was also a ship that died, not of shame but with honour. The destroyer that had given the world's Press a field day with her daring dash into Jossingfjord was laid down at the Vickers-Armstrong yard on the Tyne in June 1936, and was commissioned in June 1938.

One of the Tribal class destroyers, she had a distinguished career. She was in the Mediterranean when the war broke out and was soon on patrol off Crete before beginning her first convoy escort duty in September. It was in the middle of January 1940, when Captain Philip Vian took command, just in time to be in the thick of things for the *Altmark* episode.

Captain Vian went back to his former ship, the *Afridi*, also a Tribal class destroyer, after the *Altmark* affair, but returned to take command again in May 1940, remaining until July 1941. It was only a short time afterwards that the *Cossack* met her end.

The *Cossack* was once more helping to shepherd convoys, herding stragglers like some sheepdog and keeping ever alert for the enemy. She sailed from Gibraltar in October 1941, with a slow convoy bound for the United Kingdom. The night of 23rd October found her at the rear of the convoy, her lookouts alert for any signs of U-boats.

Suddenly, there was a terrific explosion just forward of the bridge. The destroyer had been sighted by the *U-563*. The *Cossack*'s commander, Captain E. L. Berthon, was killed, along with 158 of his officers and men. Twenty-nine were also injured. The survivors abandoned ship.

It seemed goodbye to the *Cossack*, but the destroyer was not willing to go without a fight. Members of the crew watching from the other escorts that had picked them up saw she was still afloat and that the fire started by the explosion had gone out. There seemed a chance that the *Cossack* might be saved, and she was reboarded. Some success was achieved in getting the engines going, but speed was much reduced. The battle to save this gallant ship went on for almost three days. A tug was despatched from Gibraltar, but the chances of getting the *Cossack* to safety now seemed slim as the weather got up and the destroyer rolled in the worsening conditions. It was no longer safe for the men to remain on board and they were taken off.

Dawn the following day saw the *Cossack* making her last valiant efforts to stay afloat. It was no use, and the ship that had brought rescue to the *Altmark* prisoners and written another historic chapter in the annals of the Royal Navy took her final plunge later that day.

She was a famous ship and had had a famous captain in Vian, who was in due course to become Admiral of the Fleet Sir Philip Vian. He was honoured in his own country, but the long arm of the *Altmark* episode reached out after the war, reminding him that the Norwegians had not forgotten that night in Jossingfjord.

He was cruising with the Home Fleet in Norwegian waters in 1950 and decided to ask permission to visit Jossingfjord in a destroyer. He had seen the fjord in darkness, illuminated only by the flash of searchlights, and now wished to see it in the light of day. It was not to be, the Norwegians refusing permission. This was despite the help he had given the Norwegians in their struggle against the German invaders. He had carried out an operation at Spitsbergen and even received a Norwegian order for his part in it. All this made no difference when he made his plea to see the fjord.

Sir Philip Vian, or "Vian of the *Cossack*", as he was ever afterwards to be known, died in May 1968, aged seventy-three.

The story of the *Cossack* will always be recalled whenever daring deeds of the Royal Navy are discussed. The *Cossack* was avenged when the submarine that placed the fatal torpedo in her, the *U-563*, was herself sent to the bottom by aircraft in the Bay of Biscay in 1943.

The second-in-command of the *Cossack*, Lieutenant-Commander Bradwell Talbot Turner, leader of the boarding party, gained further distinction after the war, being Naval Attaché in Oslo from 1954–7. He retired from the Royal Navy in 1957 with the rank of commander.

References to the boarding incident in Jossingfjord always attribute the famous cry "The Navy's here!", made as the hatches were flung back, to Commander Turner. Everyone seems to have accepted that it was he who made it. He has modestly refuted this, saying that it was actually shouted down another hatch by one of the ratings in the boarding party. No matter who made it, the fact remains that those words gripped the free world and are remembered to this day. "The Navy's here!" captured people's imagination, and even today there is a special ring about it.

The men from the various merchant ships sunk by the *Graf Spee* went back to sea in other ships, some to lose their lives there. One of these was Archibald Willis, second mate of the *Doric Star*, who did the drawings of pin-ups on the back of the chart on which the *Altmark*'s voyage from the South Atlantic was plotted in secret. He lost his life on his next trip to sea and never had the opportunity to put to full use his obvious talent as an artist.

Wally Wells, of Hobart, Tasmania, seventh engineer of the *Tairoa*, was more fortunate. He survived the war, and after his release from the *Altmark* wrote to his parents in Hobart, Mr and Mrs Frank Wells.

"The reports about the 'hell-ship' *Altmark* are grossly exaggerated," he said. "Things were pretty tough and everything was done to break our spirits. It was all useless and all hands remained healthy and happy and cheerful right up to the rescue." He kept an account of his experiences in the *Altmark*, and his collection of material relating to the incident is now in Hobart Maritime Museum. He died in Tasmania in 1976.

A quirk of fate prevented Melville-Evans, third mate of the *Doric Star*, from joining the ship he wanted not many months after his release from the *Altmark*, and almost certainly saved his life. The vessel he wished to join was the 15,501-ton *Arandora Star*, one of five sister ships completed for the Blue Star Line in the late 1920s. She was the last of her class to be completed and was launched in January 1927, by Cammell, Laird and Company, Ltd, Birkenhead, as the *Arandora*. She entered service on the London-La Plata service, but in 1928–9 was refitted as a cruise liner and her tonnage increased. She was renamed *Arandora Star*. Five years later, she was again refitted and her tonnage increased, finally being rebuilt in 1936 and her tonnage increased to 15,501.

Melville-Evans joined her in 1938 before transferring to the *Doric Star* during that year. He was impressed with the *Arandora Star*, which took people on cruises long before the days when cruises and fly/cruises were to become a normal thing for people who would once have considered themselves lucky to manage a week by the seaside.

The *Arandora Star*'s cruising days were now over. In December 1939, she was requisitioned by the Admiralty for service as an experimental ship for anti-torpedo nets, but at the end of June 1940, was selected for service as a troop transport.

It was in this capacity that another link with the *Graf Spee* and the *Altmark* was forged. The chief officer of the *Doric Star*, Stanley Ranson, had been released from the *Graf Spee* at Montevideo, and now found himself serving in the *Arandora Star*. Melville-Evans learned of this, and having a great respect for the man who had shared in the exciting encounter with the *Graf Spee*, thought he would like to join him in the former cruise ship. He inquired about a vacancy for an officer and was disappointed when told that it had been filled only the previous day.

The ship sailed for Canada carrying 1,500 enemy aliens on their way to internment camps in Canada. She was torpedoed seventy-five miles west of Bloody Foreland, Ireland, with heavy loss of life. Ranson was among those who perished.

Survivors gave graphic accounts of the harrowing scenes that followed when the torpedo struck home on that day, 2nd July 1940. The captain and some of the officers were still on the bridge when she went down. Men were clinging to every conceivable floating object, and the deck was a sea of faces as she sank. Windlasses and other objects rolled into the crowd of men as she made her final heel over. "The cloud of steam rose a hundred feet into the air, and the suction dragged rafts and men underneath with her. I shall never forget those horrors," one survivor was quoted as saying.

A Sunderland flying boat of Coastal Command came upon the scene and dropped first-aid kits, food, emergency rations, cigarettes and tobacco to the men waving to her from lifeboats and rafts. The flying boat then went in search of help.

The German High Command put out a communiqué which stated: "A submarine has torpedoed an armed merchantman, *Arandora Star*, off the Northern Channel."

The submarine was none other than the famed *U-47* with Lieutenant Gunther Prien in command. Prien, who, also in *U-47*, sank the battleship *Royal Oak* at Scapa Flow early in the war, had one torpedo left and was in the North Channel when the *Arandora Star* was spotted. He made no mistake with that last missile. His mistake was in not knowing that in claiming the *Arandora Star* to boost his tonnage of sinkings, he had condemned many of his fellow countrymen and Italians to their deaths.

Prien was not to survive another twelve months of the relentless war at sea. The dashing U-boat ace, his crew and *U-47* vanished forever beneath the North Atlantic in March 1941, following a pattern of depth charges from the destroyer H.M.S. *Wolverine*. The *U-47* had been stalking a convoy. The *Arandora Star* and the former chief officer of the *Doric Star* had been avenged.

Melville-Evans, thankful that he had been too late to get the position in the *Arandora Star*, continued at sea, serving in various ships. He escaped the fate of so many of his comrades, but had one eye injured by bomb blast in Tobruk Harbour. It was because of this and the high standards of eyesight required for Merchant Navy navigating officers that he subsequently left the sea and took up farming in Angus, Scotland.

Epilogue

A fine Sunday morning in February. There is a hint of spring in the air and the Angus countryside has a warmer look than is normal for so early in the year in that part of Scotland. The farmhouse home of William Melville-Evans, former third officer of the *Doric Star*, Clearbank House, Stracathro, near Brechin, has a nautical look. There are Sea Cadets and members of the Girls' Nautical Training Corps on duty to help attend to the many guests arriving by car.

This is a day to remember. For it is forty years exactly since the prisoners of the *Altmark* were rescued in Jossingfjord by H.M.S. *Cossack*. The wastes of the South Atlantic are thousands of miles away, where also rest the remains of the ships sunk by the *Graf Spee*. The icy Norwegian fjord where the last act of the drama was played out is now its normal peaceful self. A lot of those who helped shape the legend are now dead, some having died in the war.

It was to commemorate the incident and to remember the men involved that Melville-Evans decided that now, forty years on, there should be a gathering finally to set the seal on an event that has held men's interest through the decades that have passed since then.

It was his original intention to hold the reunion at Jossingfjord, but illness prevented him from carrying out this plan. He felt that there must be a reunion, come what may, and decided that in the circumstances the best place would be his home. He set about arranging matters with his usual thoroughness, seeking to have the reunion as representative as possible. He had earlier visited Jossingfjord and met villagers there, making friends among them. He wanted Norwegians to be present at the ceremony, and also invited Captain Walter Schmidt, the third officer of the *Altmark*, and his wife.

No reunion could be complete without the Royal Navy being represented. Melville-Evans wished to have a link with H.M.S. *Cossack* if possible, and in this respect was fortunate in that Vice-Admiral Sir Hector MacLean, who was navigating officer in the *Cossack* at the time, promised to attend. Lord Mackie of Benshie also accepted his invitation. Norwegians from Jossingfjord also looked forward to being present, as did Walter Schmidt and Mrs Schmidt.

The date and time were fixed, Sunday, 17th February 1980, at twelve noon at Clearbank House—exactly forty years since the prisoners freed from the *Altmark* arrived at Leith.

The never-to-be-forgotten day dawned, and the many guests began to arrive at Melville-Evans' home, with its permanent links with the sea, the Red Ensign, a pilot "jack" and a ship's bell, at the entrance. Guests were not "piped aboard", but they were greeted on arrival by a smart salute from Stonehaven Unit Sea Cadet Corps, under Lieutenant-Commander Robin Walker. Vice-Admiral Sir Hector MacLean arrived—he retired from the Royal Navy in 1962—as did several Norwegians from Jossingfjord, one of them presenting Mr Melville-Evans with a pewter bowl to mark the occasion. Among those who also attended was a delegation of the Inter-Parliamentary Union from Luxembourg.

The one man Melville-Evans was anxious should be there—for they had shared so much of the episode—was unable to be present. Travel difficulties prevented Walter Schmidt and Mrs Schmidt from being able to attend. They had met previously at Melville-Evans' home, but it was a sad disappointment that they should be prevented from being together at this first and final reunion of those associated with the *Altmark* affair.

The absence of the former third officer of the *Altmark* was the only disappointing note in an event that otherwise went ahead without a hitch. Sea Cadets who were not even born when the *Cossack* made her dash into the fjord were proud to have a link with the Royal Navy when they were inspected by Vice-Admiral Sir Hector MacLean, and the White Ensign run up.

The day, of course, belonged to those who had actually taken part in the *Altmark* episode, whether as British, German or Norwegian, and the toast of "Seamen All", proposed by Lord Mackie of Benshie, was a fitting tribute to them.

For there were neither heroes nor cowards in the saga of the *Altmark*—just men of different nationalities thrown together for a brief moment in time who, through adversity, learned mutual respect and that men, no matter under which flag they may serve, are linked by the common bond of humanity. They were, in the end, just "Seamen All".

Appendix 1

Prisoners released from the *Altmark* by the *Cossack* were:

ASHLEA: R. Goss, 2nd offcr, R. K. Miller, 3rd offcr, A. Jack, 2nd engr, W. T. Hair, 3rd engr, A. E. Walker, 4th engr, P. K. J. Warren, cadet. Olde, T., Harris, T., Dixon, C., Everitt, T., Robinson, G., Campbell, S. J., Coran, J., McCaffrey, Rockett, J. W., Young, C., Bevan, N., Ardell, D., Talbart, Jusen, Macritchie, D., Macalinden, M., Ritchie, R., Francisco, J. H., Benjamin, C. B., Davis, T., Mangun, C., Borge, E. A., Guy, J., Earl, S., Dumbe, W.

DORIC STAR: F. Wall, asst engr, A. E. Willis, 2nd offcr, W. Evans, 3rd offcr, L. R. Vandone, sen. engr, H. E. Gandy, ch. std, A. J. Walls, asst engr, P. Bowie, asst engr, T. J. Layton, jun. 3rd engr, A. C. Watt, asst engr, R. A. Curtis, 3rd engr, N. Watson, asst, engr, G. A. King, 2nd engr, H. W. Jones, 4th engr, Dykes, J., Baker, L. G., Mitchell, J. H., Ferguson, S., Turnbull, J., Pilskala, A., Foley, T., Curtis, W., Robinson, V., Ward, B. G., Lovely, J., Softley, J., Hyde, T., Clark, A., Flowers, S., Synch, J., McSween, Dolphin, A., Miller, D., Alen, J., Jenkins, Wright, J., Kingston, D., Kilross, J., Roberts, W., Harris, R., McGirley, C., Bones, F., Plummer, C., Soderbloom, C., Clark, L. W., Lovely, J. E., Hall, E., Moffitt, K., Wilkinson, J., Ashton, E. J., Wheeler, W., Marshman, R., Grimas, Bloomer, A., McManus, Underwood, Garwood.

HUNTSMAN: Captain A. H. Brown, A. A. Johnson, 2nd offcr, A. Creer, 2nd engr, E. S. Hall, 3rd engr, F. Cluny, 4th engr, B. A. Lyons, 5th engr, L. Frost, 3rd offcr, P. Appleby, ch.std, Carr, J., Goldstein. A., Hughes, H., Wreight, H. H., Macintyre, G., Aledool Jolill, Wasiur Rahman, Ali Ahmad, Sultan Ahamod, Umoor Meah, Abdul Wahale, Reazuddin, Ali Hussian, Sultan Ahmad, Abdul Ahmad, Reazulle, Somodeali, Jaburulle, Meadon, Monoroozulle, Eusuphulla, Pasadullah, Tormoozullah, Edrisulle, Khurshidali,

Munsoorali, Woolfatulla, Yeasimullah, Mansoorali, Arfanulle, Harisulle, Mofizali, Sunaulle, Gonoomian, Shakuroollah, Kala Mian, Sahebali, Badiuzzaman, Sk Edoo, Mahdmeah, Ana Meah, Amir Ali, Syed Ahmad, Munshi Mian, Sultan Ahamad, Noor Ahmad, Badsha Mian, Kanai, Sorafathali, Thacoordhone, Muntazunam, Massimulle, Zauil Abdin, Komoreallee, Sumshireullah, Asmanali, Forasatulle, Luckmanullah, Konaullah, Ramganali, Noimoolle, Reasutulla, Untorali, Hashmatullah, Harishmeah, Sekander Mian, Somodeulle, Shearazlli Hawk, Asadulle, Abdul Azis, Mungli, Mahd Essack.

NEWTON BEECH: W. M. Woodman, 2nd mate, G. H. Byrne, 3rd mate, H. Savill, 2nd engr, S. Smith, 3rd engr, T. Northey, 4th engr, T. W. Hunter, app., R. Atkinson, cadet, Abel, R., Swaby, J., Moody, A., Miller, L. R., Reay, C. M. S., Williams, S., Morrison, D., Martin, A., Wardell, A., Johnson, G., Zerk, L. F. A., O'Connor, M., Gilleard, W., Bell, J., Smith, T., Campbell, W., Hanlon, P., Angus, A., Bowler, W., Beattie, G., Holland, H., White, A. W., Worsey, G. D.

TAIROA: Captain W. B. Starr, R. A. Costa, 2nd offcr, F. J. Patterson, 3rd offcr, J. Bammant, 4th offcr, F. L. Keen, extra offcr, J. L. Naylor, 2nd engr, C. W. Taylor, 3rd engr, N. K. Brown, 4th engr, I. F. Hunter, 5th engr, A. Ketley, 6th engr, T. W. Rowell, engr, W. F. Wells, 7th engr, J. C. Smith, ch.std., Stone, R. H., Connaughton, P. J., Langhelt, F., Newton, A., Hall, C. W., Macminne, W. E., McMillan, D., Robinson, W., Maclead, D., Shorland, H., Gordon, J., Olsson, F., Barker, J., Tanner, T., Gant, A., Poysden, H., Gosling, D., Summers, J., Miller, W. G., Whelan, A. J., Southeard, L. C., Blakeman, W., Hill, F., Guthrie, N., Pemberton, S., Webb, J. C., Phelan, V., Macarthy, J., Quigley, A., Downey, R., Blithe, J., Grant, T. C. E., Arter, D., McDonald, T. C., Moran, J., Pittan, R., Bannon, J., Rowsell, S. J., Hansen, J. W. R., Reynolds, J., Oakley, J., Adamson, L., Matthews, T., Payne, T., O'Toole, M., Nichols, D., Evans, G. K., Daly, J. E., Lindberg, A., Rogers, H. Tynemouth, T., Macwhinney, S., Langley, H., Keating, J., Wightman, T., O'Brien, P., Purvis, N. J., Cook, D. W., Hall, C. W., Wilkens, J., Hoban, M., Stark, F. C.

TREVANION: W. H. Platten, 2nd offcr, R. Cudbertson, 3rd offcr, H. J. Burrows, 2nd engr, E. G. Elcock, 3rd engr, J. C. Scott, 4th engr, G. C. Barrett, 5th engr, E. Spiers, 6th engr, P. Filceck, cadet, A. N.

Smith, Cadet, J. O. Symons, ch.std, Warwick, T. J., Leigh, J. A., Riley, W., Morgan, T., Kennedy, M., Lery, W., Hunt, J., Thomas, Lafferty, Rogers, P., Burns, R., Stewart, W. G., Flannagan, J., Baker, R., Surtees, R., Mannesson, J., Jaland, Howli, Palmer, J.

Appendix 2

This was the statement, as spelt, handed to the captains of merchant ships by the officer in charge of the boarding party each time the *Admiral Graf Spee* intercepted a vessel:

The German government and people wish ardently to live in peace with the english people. There are no questions which could not be solved and settled by negotiations.

But, because your government declared war, we are obliged to save our honor and living.

There beeing war between our nations, I am obliged, to take your ship over as prize.

From reasons of humanity J will do all J can, to save the lifes and personal propertie of your crew.

Jt will possible only on one condition. *You have to obey without active or passive resistance to all orders, given by the german officers*, J will put on boad your ship to take over command. Jn case of any resistance J regrette to be forced to destroy your ship instantly. Jn that case J refuse all responsibility for any injury or loss. That responsibility will be exclusively Yours.

Bibliography

The Second World War, Volume I *The Gathering Storm*, Winston S. Churchill, Cassell, 1948.

The Battle of the River Plate, Dudley Pope, Wm Kimber & Co. Ltd, London, 1956.

The Navy's Here, The Altmark Affair, Willi Frischeuer and Robert Jackson, Victor Gollancz, Ltd, London, 1955.

The Tribals, Martin H. Brice, Ian Allan, London, 1971.

Action This Day, Admiral of the Fleet Sir Philip Vian, Frederick Muller, London, 1960.

Hitler's Naval War, Cajus Bekker, Macdonald and Jane, London, 1974.

The German Navy in World War II, Edward P. Von der Porten, Arthur Barker, London, 1970.

The Secret Raiders, David Woodward, Wm Kimber & Co. Ltd, London, 1955.

Subs and Submariners, Arch Whitehouse, Frederick Muller, London, 1963.

Sjoforsvarets noytralitetsvern 1939–1940 Tysklands og Vestmaktenes planer og forberedelser for en Norgesaksjon, E. A. Steen, Utgitt Ved Den Krigshistoriske Avdeling.

Altmark-Saken 1940, Reidar Omang, Gyldendal Norsk Forlag, Oslo, 1953.

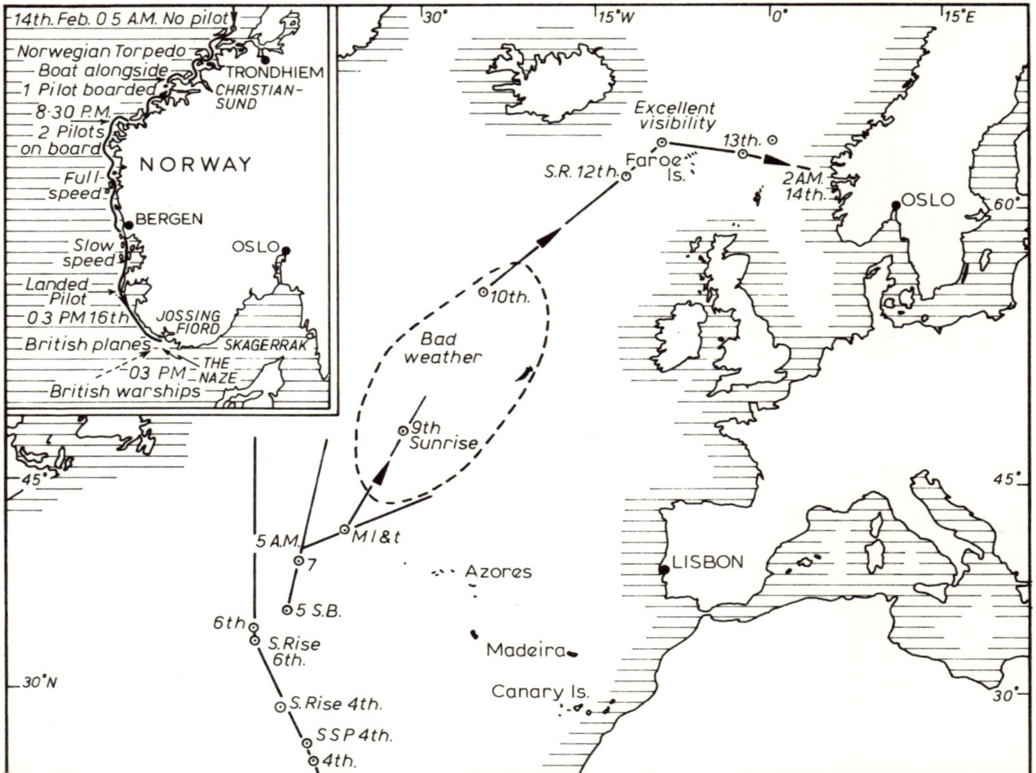
14th. Feb. 0 5 A.M. No pilot
Norwegian Torpedo Boat alongside
1 Pilot boarded
8·30 P.M.
2 Pilots on board
NORWAY
TRONDHIEM
CHRISTIAN-SUND
Full-speed
BERGEN
Slow speed
OSLO
Landed Pilot
0 3 PM 16th
JOSSING FIORD
SKAGERRAK
British planes
03 PM
THE NAZE
British warships
30°
15°W
0°
15°E
Excellent visibility
13th.
Faroe Is.
S.R. 12th.
2AM. 14th.
OSLO
60°
10th.
Bad weather
9th Sunrise
M I & t
5 A.M.
7
5 S.B.
6th
S. Rise 6th.
S. Rise 4th.
S S P 4th.
4th.
Azores
Madeira
Canary Is.
LISBON
45°
30°N
30°

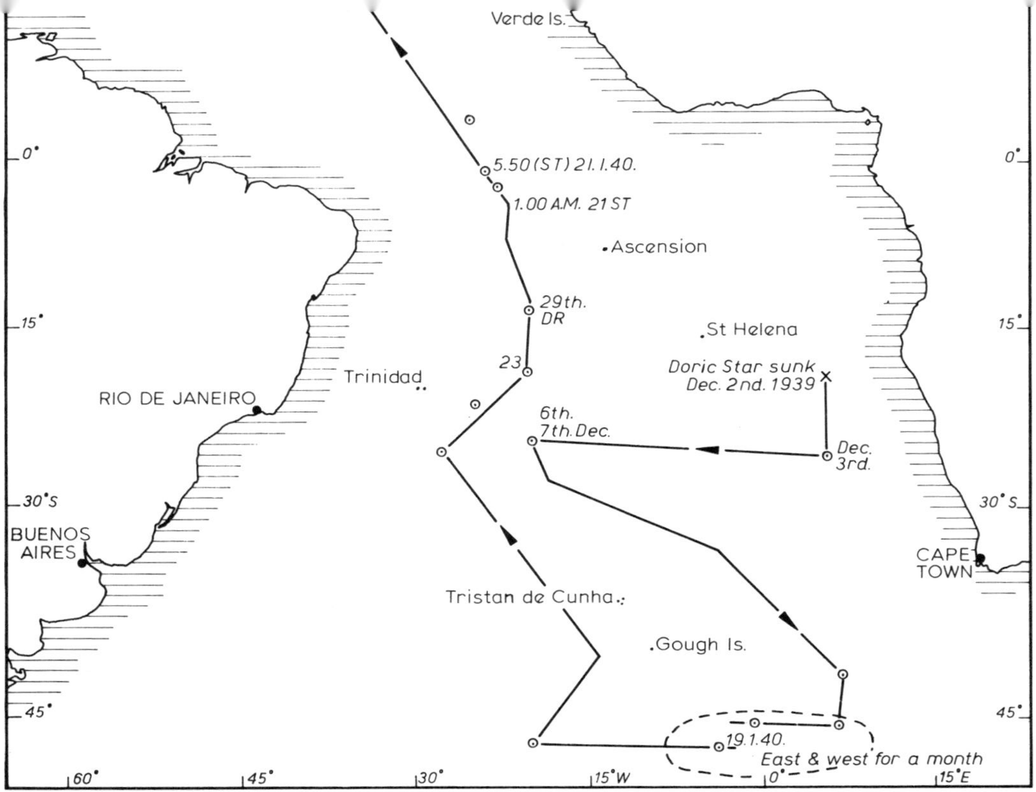
Verde Is.
5.50 (ST) 21.1.40.
1.00 A.M. 21 ST
Ascension
29th.
DR
St Helena
23
Doric Star sunk
Dec. 2nd. 1939
Trinidad
RIO DE JANEIRO
6th.
7th. Dec.
Dec.
3rd.
BUENOS
AIRES
CAPE
TOWN
Tristan de Cunha
Gough Is.
19.1.40.
East & west for a month
0°
15°
30° S
45°
60°
45°
30°
15° W
0°
15° E

Index